Gary's Guide to

Successful Book Signings

Including tips, tricks, and anecdotes from experienced authors and booksellers

Gary's Guide to Successful Book Signings

Including tips, tricks, and anecdotes from experienced authors and booksellers

Gary D. Robson

Proseyr Publishing
Red Lodge, MT   U.S.A.

Gary's Guide to Successful Book Signings
By Gary D. Robson

Body copy set in Book Antiqua
Headings set in Avenir Next

First edition
ISBN 978-0-9659609-8-4 (paperback)

Proseyr Publishing
PO Box 1630, Red Lodge, MT 59068
www.proseyr.com

*To my amazingly supportive
and understanding wife, Kathy.
Thank you for putting up with
being married to a writer.*

Contents

Gary D. Robson

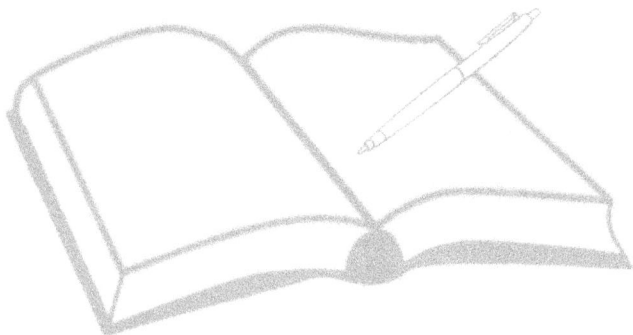

I did not write this book by myself. Other authors and booksellers contributed the tips, tricks, and anecdotes that pepper this book—in more ways than one! Their words are peppered (scattered) throughout the book and they pepper (spice up) everything I have to say. I could not have done it without their help; let me offer a huge thank you to:

C.B. Bernard

Lynn Boughey

John Clayton

Margaret Coel

Sneed B. Collard III

Gary Ferguson

Kevin Gascoyne

Drew Goodman

James W. Hall

Janet Muirhead Hill

Ed Kemmick

Carrie La Seur

Craig Lancaster

Elisa Lorello

Keith McCafferty

Vonda McIntyre

Scott McMillion

Douglas Preston

Bruce Raisch

Susan Kushner Resnick

Chrysti "the Wordsmith" Smith

ACKNOWLEDGEMENTS

Gary D. Robson

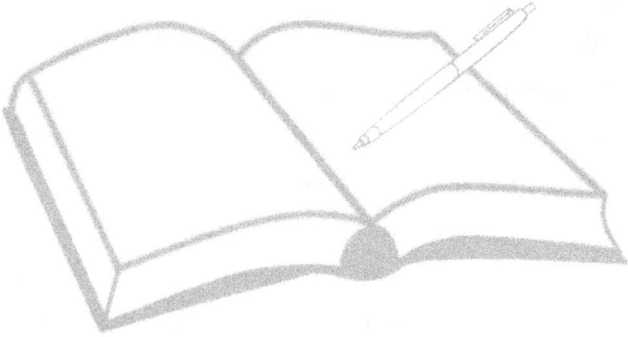

I have been writing books for a long time now, starting with computer software manuals in the 1980s, and moving on to children's books, technical books, historical fiction, and more.

As excited as I was when that first manual was done (it was a thrilling page-turner about your brand-new external hard disk!), I soon discovered that most of the world doesn't consider product manuals to be "real" books. Nobody does book signings for computer manuals. Most software these days doesn't even come with a manual.

When my first "real" book came out, I gleefully began arranging book signings and other events for it.

I sat at tables in hotel lobbies at conventions selling books. I gave talks at trade shows and signed books afterward in the back of the room. Each new book I wrote required a different strategy for book events. I did book signings and talks in gift shops, libraries, department stores, schools, museums, National Park lodges, trade show booths, wildlife sanctuaries, outdoor fairs, and even the occasional bookstore.

Some events drew wonderful crowds—and correspondingly wonderful book sales. Other events consisted of sitting by myself at a table, surrounded by books and staring off into space.

In 2001, I bought The Broadway Bookstore in Red Lodge, Montana (which I later renamed Red Lodge Books & Tea), and got a very different perspective on book signings. As I brought in authors, I watched what they did. Sometimes I learned from them; sometimes I taught them. Most of the time I did both.

At first, I was convinced there was a pattern. There must be some magic formula that would assure success for every event. I know now that there is no such formula. On the other hand, there are little things you can do that make success more (or less) likely.

The more events I was involved in, the more patterns started to emerge. I noted what seemed to help or hurt, and eventually started writing about them on my blog, GaryDRobson.com. These quickly became the most popular articles on the site, except for one blog post about Corriente cattle. I have no idea why so many people read that post. Even cattle ranchers typically don't know what a Corriente is. I had to write the Wikipedia page myself. (Hmm. Maybe that's another book idea...)

In this book, I've gathered together everything I have learned from all of these book signing events. I realize, however, that there are a lot of people who have done more (and better) events than I have, so I reached out to other authors and booksellers that I've met over the years and asked for their tips and anecdotes.

For those who like to skip straight to the last page of the mystery novel to see whodunit, let me summarize the book in three words: communication, attitude, preparation.

Book signings go better if the author and the venue communicate before, during, and after the event; the author maintains a positive attitude throughout the process, even (especially) if things go badly; and everyone involved prepares for the event beforehand.

Whether you are an author, a bookseller, a conference organizer, or a shopkeeper, I hope that this book will help you to run book events that benefit everybody involved. If you have experiences of your own to share, let me know. There may be a second edition down the road!

Promotion & Planning

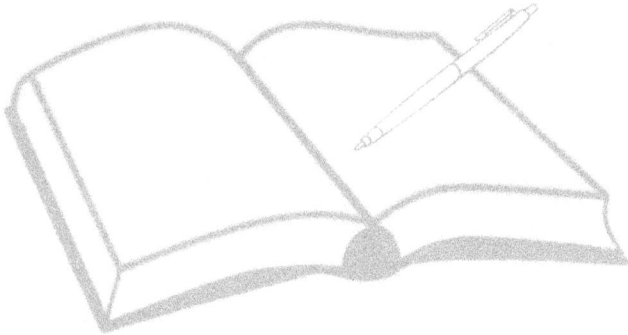

At long last, your book is done. You've handed off the final manuscript to your editor, had your photo taken for the book jacket, and emptied your celebratory bottle of wine. The publisher (and proofreader and editor and cover designer and...) can take it from here. Time to start on the next book?

No. It's time to start planning the marketing and promotion for *this* book!

Whether you're self-published or published by one of the big houses, the success of your book depends on your marketing efforts. Alas, publishing houses don't have the budgets and staffing for promotion that they used to have. It's up to you to pick up the slack.

It's easy to get caught up in the simple things that you can do at home in your pajamas, like press releases, an author website, and a Facebook page for the book. Granted, those are all important tasks that need to be handled, but they probably shouldn't be your highest priority at this point. Focus on things that need to be done well in advance, such as scheduling book signings.

If you're an author, you probably have a website and/or a blog. You're probably on Facebook, Twitter, Instagram, Pinterest, or other social media. You probably send out an e-newsletter. (If you're not doing any of these things, why not?) Once you've finalized the schedule for a book signing, tell everyone about it! Help the bookstore spread the word. It's your book, and nobody can talk about it better than you can.

Editors and agents look for their authors to have what they call a "platform," which previous generations might have called a soapbox. Your platform is the collection of fans, readers, followers, and potential book buyers that you can reach directly.

It's not always the obvious things, like the aforementioned social media. Your platform might include listeners on a podcast where you guest host, subscribers to your YouTube channel, people who go to your open mic performances, or regular readers of your column.

If this isn't your first book, your platform includes readers of your previous books. If you are an expert in a particular field, your platform includes anyone who reads your articles or papers and anyone who attends your lectures.

There are certain promotional tasks that are usually done by authors and publishers, and others that are usually done by the bookstore or other venue. The problem is that there's no hard, fast set of rules. The only way to make a signing effective is for the author and the venue to work out in advance who is doing what.

Develop a look

There are an awful lot of authors out there, and it's hard to stand out. It's even harder if you look different every time someone sees you.

Gary D. Robson

Pick a look—or persona, if you prefer—that you like, that fits both you and the books you write. If you write Westerns, grab a cowboy hat and boots. If you write business books, a nice suit is more appropriate. Once you've selected that look, have some author photos taken.

Use the photos that fit the look on all of your social media and book covers, and dress that way for your live events.

Make sure your look is compatible with your book design. If you write goth vampire mysteries, don't wear a frilly sun dress and sandals for your author photo.

People may not always recognize your face, but they're much more likely to remember your total look.

Email

It's usually best if both author and publisher do emails. Your lists probably don't overlap much, so you'll get a broader reach if you use both.

Press kits

A press kit for a book generally contains a brief description of the book, a brief bio of the author, a nice crisp author photo, a hi-res image of the book cover, and some details about the book, like the full title, publisher, ISBN/EAN, page count, physical size, binding type, author's website, and a list of distributors that carry the book.

Sometimes, especially with new authors, I have a devil of a time finding a good hi-res photo of the author or the book cover to use on our posters and announcements. Let me pause for a moment here to define "hi-res."

Digital photos have both a size (like "2 by 3 inches") and a resolution (like "300 dpi"). DPI stands for "dots per inch." What matters when you're blowing a picture up for a sign is the total dot count. A 2x3 picture at 300 dpi (hi-res) is 600x900 dots, but at 50 dpi (low-res) it's only 100x150 dots.

This picture from one of John Cameron's book signings at two different resolutions should make the difference clear:

The picture on the left is 300dpi and the one on the right is 50dpi.

If you're not sure how to size your pictures correctly, send them at full resolution, or have someone help you. A good sharp author picture is important.

When you confirm the signing, ask the store manager if a press kit would be useful. If you have any little giveaways, like buttons or bookmarks, send some in advance for the bookstore's promotional display.

If you create a generic poster, make sure it has space for the store name, contact information, and event time and date.

Make sure that the poster does not encourage people to buy somewhere else. I've had authors send me a lovely poster with our event information on it that said "Available at Amazon.com" right on the poster. I think I speak for all bookstores when I say a sign is not going on my window if it tells my customers to buy from a competitor!

Gary D. Robson

If you have friends in the city you're going to be signing in, by all means contact them via email (from three to five days ahead of the event), as well as the usual post on Facebook and Twitter. It can also work, depending on the book, to write a useful, topical piece for the local newspaper, to appear in the same week of the signing, ending with a third-person line about the signing. (i.e. Gary Ferguson will be signing copies of...).

Gary Ferguson, author of over a dozen books, including *The Carry Home*, *Through the Woods*, and *Hawks Rest*.

Press releases

Unlike a press kit, a press release is a simple announcement about your book. I like to tailor them to the event and the venue. If you've appeared in that store before, say "Susan is returning to Downtown Books" instead of "Susan is speaking at Downtown Books." If you live in the area, mention that.

There is some disagreement in the business about whether press releases should come from the author, the publisher, or the venue. I think the author should always be involved, but if there's a professional publicist available to write the press release, let them do it! It's what they do for a living, and they know how to write a press release that will get printed.

Some newspapers take the attitude that if a store owner wants to promote events, he can buy an ad. In this case, a press release from the author might sound more like "news" and less like advertising. In other cases, the store might have a good working relationship with the paper, and the author will want to take advantage of it.

Don't forget that press releases aren't only for newspapers. They may get picked up by radio and TV or specialty newsletters.

Is your book about surviving cancer? Send a press release to the local chapter of the American Cancer Society and the local support groups. Is it a political book? Send one to the local party headquarters. Press releases are cheap. Don't skimp.

Talk shows

This is all on the author. Nobody wants to turn on the radio and listen to someone from a bookstore talk about a new book; people want to hear from the author. Getting an interview on the morning radio show or TV news the day of the book signing makes a huge difference in attendance.

This isn't as daunting as it may sound. In small towns, a press release or a phone call sent to the studio is often all it takes. Just make sure your pitch starts with the local angle. If you tell a radio station in Idaho that you're a Florida author calling to talk about your new book, they won't care. But if you tell them that you're an author visiting Boise, Idaho Falls, Pocatello, and Coeur d'Alene next week, they will probably listen to the rest of the pitch.

Facebook

Facebook is still the 500-pound gorilla in the room when it comes to social media. If you don't already have a Facebook account, create one.

Facebook has two different ways to put yourself out there: the personal profile and the fan page.

The personal profile is the core of Facebook. Connections are two-way: people send you friend requests, and you choose to accept or ignore them. Many Facebook users have their entire personal life spewed across their personal profile, but you don't have to do that. For most authors, it's better if you don't do that.

A page is more open. Anyone can click the "like" button to follow the page. You can control the amount of interactivity your fans have; settings allow or deny fans the ability to post on the page's timeline, add photos and videos, tag the photos on the page, and so forth.

Personal profiles are for friends; pages are for fans.

One profile can have multiple pages. If you write in more than one genre, you can set up a profile and then create a fan page for your children's books and another for your romance novels; those will be two very different pages!

Unfortunately, it can be difficult for posts on a fan page to be noticed. Based on my experiments, if you create a page for your book and get 1,000 "likes," only 100 to 150 of those people will actually see the things you post, although there are some ways to increase that number.

Luckily for you, Facebook has the perfect way to promote a book event. They call it an "event page." When you tell Facebook you wish to create an event, it will ask for a title, description, date, time, and so forth. Make sure to fill in all of the details; that will help Internet search engines to find it. Also, make sure you link to your website or blog.

It will also give you the opportunity to upload an event banner. Do this! Pictures get much more attention than straight text on social media.

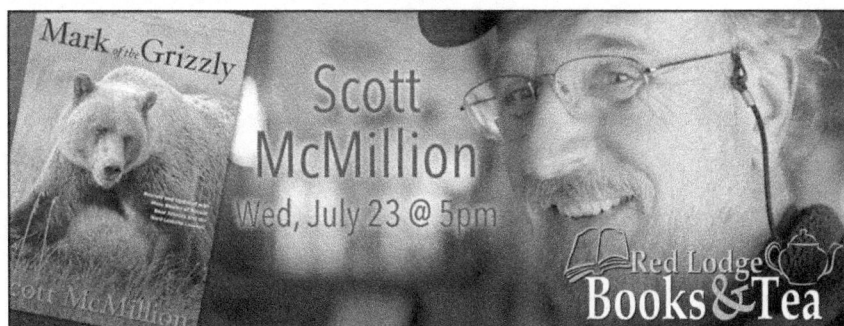

This banner for a Scott McMillion signing includes two important visual elements: the book cover and an author photo. It also includes the author name, event location, book title, and the date & time of the event, even though that information is all in the event description. Why? Because people look at pictures before they read text, and sometimes people will link or share the picture somewhere other than Facebook, losing the associated description.

Here's another example of an event banner:

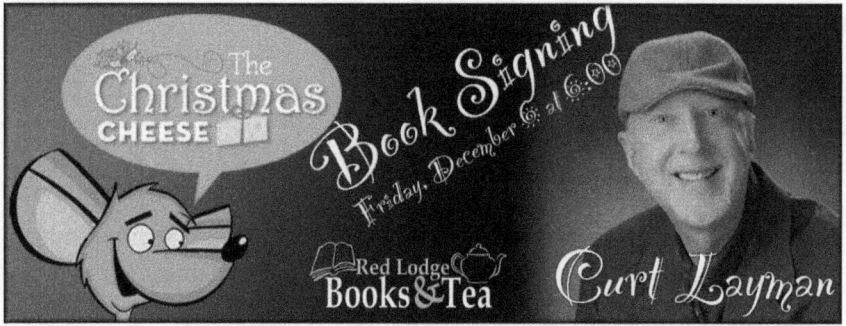

This one is for a heavily illustrated book, and we felt that the illustration style was more important than the cover image, so we extracted the mouse picture and highlighted that instead.

If you don't have a way to create an attractive banner yourself, either have a friend with Facebook do it for you or just use a picture of the book cover. Either way, make sure you have a banner picture!

Once you've created the event, set yourself up as the host, along with the location where the event will be held. Then start inviting people. Every person you invite will get a notification that you've invited them to an event. As long as you've set the event to "public," every time one of them accepts the invitation, Facebook will announce that on their timeline ("Gary is attending Book Signing with Curt Layman"), and all of their friends will see it. Ask your friends to please share the event. The more people share it, like it, or declare that they are attending, the higher Facebook pushes the event on timelines.

The author and publisher shouldn't make two competing event pages. Decide who will create it, and then let everybody invite people to join.

Algorithms on Facebook tend to make posts more visible when people interact with them (clicking "like," making comments, or sharing the post). You'll do better if one of you makes an announcement and the other shares it. And always include a picture. It dramatically increases the number of people who read and respond.

Don't just set up the event page and then leave it alone. Check to see if people have posted questions. Post something to the event timeline every now and then, whether it's a picture of the venue or the cover of the book. Everyone who has been invited, except for those who declined, will see those posts.

Twitter

Twitter and Facebook are very different animals. On Facebook, you can drone on and on at great length, but on Twitter you must cram your ten pounds of wisdom into a tiny 140-character container — even less if you include a picture or link.

The announcement of your book event on Twitter should be snappy and short, with a picture and a link to the event details elsewhere.

The flip side to not having a big static page is that you can send out multiple tweets as the event approaches. A week in advance, mention that the launch party will include cupcakes from the amazing bakery down the street. If it's an out-of-town event, tweet when you get to town. Tweet a picture of the venue. Tweet the day before to say how excited you are.

If your book gets a good review or a write-up in the press, tweet that, too. If you reply to one of your own tweets, it creates a chain, connecting the tweets for your followers. If you do this more than a few times, though, it will bury the follow-up tweets behind a "view entire conversation" link.

Your website or blog

The front page of your website or blog should list upcoming events, unless you have so many that they require a page of their own. For the launch party, write a detailed blog post about the event when it's first set up and link to the Facebook event page.

YouTube

You specialize in the written word. What possible use could you have for a video website like YouTube or Vine? You'd be surprised. Here are just a few of the things you can do to promote books on YouTube:

Book Trailers

Over the last four years, we've seen more and more publishers creating book trailers. For those not familiar with the concept, it's basically the same thing as a movie trailer. Think of it as a TV commercial for a book.

Book trailers can be funny or serious. They can feature the author reading the book, or have no spoken words at all. If you're a self-published author or your publisher doesn't do trailers, the idea of creating a trailer is pretty daunting.

Book trailers from the big publishing houses are slick productions, often using professional videographers, editors, and actors. The budget on some of these is probably bigger than your advance. But that doesn't mean you can't make your own.

Not all authors like the idea of making a video book trailer (Jonathan Franzen is a good example), but we have to recognize that YouTube isn't all cute cat videos. It's a powerful marketing tool, and book trailers are a great way to pitch your book.

Last year, I decided to give it a try. I Googled around looking for tutorials on trailers. Most focused on fairly primitive slide-show-like tools. That wasn't quite what I was after. I spend a whole day once trying to build something in Prezi, but it always looked like a Prezi presentation instead of a book trailer. Same thing with PowerPoint. No matter what I did, it always felt like a slide show.

I use a Mac, and a few years ago I spent some time working on iMovie. I was fairly unimpressed. But I watched a tutorial on PC Classes Online about the latest version, and it has improved significantly. It looked like it could get the job done, so I fired up iMovie and went to work creating a one-minute trailer for the Yellowstone book from my *Who Pooped in the Park?* series.

That trailer took me about four hours to build. I had already scanned all of the pages from the book for a PowerPoint presentation I did some years back, so that was a time-saver. I certainly wouldn't call this the equivalent of one of the big fancy children's book trailers from Penguin, but it says what I want it to say.

I'm not going to try to write an iMovie tutorial here—the video tutorial I mentioned above handles that just fine—but I'll give you some tips.

- Don't use commercial music. You value the copyright on your book, right? Then respect the copyright of the musician. You can search for free music (Freeplay Music has thousands of songs you can use on YouTube videos), use the built-in music in iMovie (I confess: that's what I did), or create music yourself. You can also do it without music.

- If you use spoken words, repeat them in subtitles or closed captions. If someone is watching your book trailer in an office or other quiet environment, they'll have the sound off. They should catch the whole message. Besides, deaf people read books, too!

- This should be obvious for writers, but proofread, proofread, proofread. And then have someone else proofread, too. It looks really bad for a book trailer to have spelling or grammatical errors.

- If you use a lot of the Ken Burns effect to pan across your pictures or pages, try to keep the motion relatively slow and steady. In retrospect, I panned too fast on some of the shots in my trailer.
- Include your website. This is a trailer for your book. Make sure people can find you!
- If your book is only available in e-book format, state that explicitly. Don't make people waste a bunch of time searching for the printed version.
- If your book is available in bookstores, say that. Don't just say "available online" or "available on Amazon."
- Once you have the trailer ready to go, put it everywhere. Create a YouTube channel. Tweet out a link. Put it on Facebook. Put it on your blog. Put it on the book's website if it has one. The trailer doesn't do any good unless people watch it.
- Keep it short and sweet. A minute is a good length. Two minutes is the absolute max for most of us. I've seen effective book trailers only 30 seconds long!
- If you use your voice, use a professional microphone. We can take some great video with cell phones these days, but you don't want your audio to sound tinny and hard to understand.
- Watch a bunch of trailers for books similar to yours to get a feeling for what people expect in your genre. I watched a lot of children's book trailers before deciding what I wanted to do with mine.
- Don't try to pack in too much information. Unless you're doing a trailer for *Goodnight Moon*, you can't do a full plot synopsis in 30 seconds. Keep it simple!
- Use the title of the book, and show the book cover.
- Don't forget to include your name, too.

Gary D. Robson

📖   Have fun! If you obsess over making the book trailer perfect, you'll never end up making one. Enjoy the process, and when it looks good enough, put it out and move on.

If you'd like to check out the trailer, just go to YouTube and search for "Who Pooped in the Park? Official Yellowstone Book Trailer."

Readings or book talks

Nobody but your mother is going to watch a half-hour video of you reading from your book. Editing together a short (2–5 minute) video from one of your readings or talks, on the other hand, could be just the thing to get someone interested in buying a copy.

Make sure the video camera or phone that you use is either on a tripod or propped securely on something that doesn't shake. If you have someone with a SteadyCam and some videography experience, that's great. Otherwise, just keep it simple.

When you're creating the footage, make sure to record the introduction. It's better to have someone else spend a few seconds telling the audience why you're wonderful than to do it yourself. You don't have to record a two-minute introduction that tells your whole life story, but something short and sweet saying who you are is perfect.

At some point in the video, make sure to include a shot of the book cover.

Gary D. Robson

Signage & Props

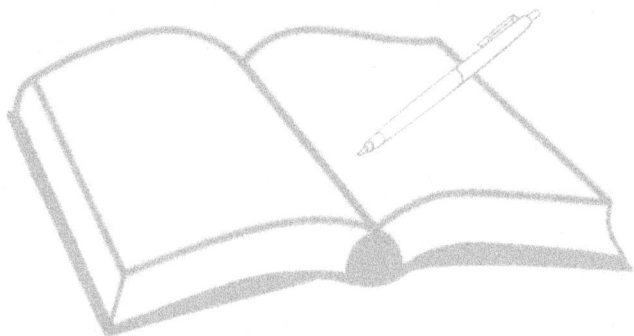

The days of huge marketing budgets at publishing companies are, alas, behind us. There are still publishers that provide posters, cardboard stand-ups, and other tools for their authors, but such tools aren't as elaborate as they used to be. Even if your publisher does have money to allocate for your book tour, you're probably better off spending it on travel and getting in a few extra locations instead of making a life-sized cardboard cutout of yourself.

Posters & signs

The first question you need to ask yourself before getting signs made is whether you'll be driving to all of your events or flying. If you fly, you want signage that's easy to get onto an airplane. Consider a lightweight folding easel with a banner that rolls up and fits in your suitcase (or in the case for the easel). Make sure desk signs and posters are small enough to lay flat in the suitcase.

If you'll be driving, you have a lot more options. This doesn't mean you should go out and buy two huge signs mounted on foam-core board and a pair of giant oak easels. First of all, you are going to have to tote all of this stuff from your car into the venue where your event takes place. If you end up having to park four blocks away, you'll regret bringing bulky or heavy accessories. Secondly, most bookstores are limited on space. I've done book signings where there was barely room for my chair, my table, and a stack of books.

Many authors don't bring signs at all, depending on the venue to provide them. That works in a bookstore where the staff is actively pointing you out and telling potential customers about you. It doesn't work so well in the corner of a gift shop or department store, where passersby have no idea who you are and why you're there, and they're probably looking for commemorative shot glasses rather than books.

A nice poster on an easel next to your chair can help a lot. It should be eye-catching, and have your name and the title of your book in big, readable text. Including the cover of the book helps, as does a picture of you.

A picture of you? But you're sitting there right next to the sign. Why would you need your picture on it?

You'll be amazed how often someone will come up, look at the sign, look at you, look back at the sign, and say something clever like, "Hey! That's you!"

Heck, I've been amazed at the number of people that look at me sitting behind a pile of books next to a sign emblazoned with my likeness, and say, "So, did you write this book?"

Hint: as tempting as it may be, do not answer that question with "Nope. I'm just the author's hair stylist, but I'd be happy to sign a book for you." That line doesn't sell many books.

Giveaways

It's always nice to have some giveaways on the table. The most common are bookmarks, which are inexpensive advertising and double as a business card that they'll keep with the book. Another common one is cookies, at least at the smaller events.

Bookmarks

Bookmarks are functional, inexpensive, and double as a marketing tool. If you decide to make bookmarks (or have your publisher make them for you), make sure to include a list of all of your books, and if you have a series, list the books in order. Many fans want to read the books in the "correct" order. You get to define what that order is, whether it's the order you wrote them or the chronological order of the storyline.

Color costs a bit more, but it's absolutely worth it.

One major faux pas to avoid on the bookmarks is information about where to buy the books. No store wants to set up an event with you and have you hand out bookmarks instructing customers to buy your books somewhere else.

Book buyers are smart people. They'll be able to figure out how to find your books using Google. If your books are in the standard distribution channels (e.g., Ingram and Baker & Taylor), then customers can go to pretty much any bookstore in the country. And putting "Available on Amazon.com" is just pointless. If you've written a book, people will assume that it's available on Amazon.

There are other low-cost options, too. Some authors do stickers, postcards, magnets, buttons, or balloons. The publisher of my children's books, Farcountry Press, made temporary tattoos, which the kids love!

Goodies

I regularly have local authors show up for their book signings bearing cookies, muffins, cupcakes, and other homemade goodies to give away. We've even had vegetable platters and cakes. Customers absolutely love it, but make sure to check with the store before bringing in treats. Some stores prefer not to have people wandering around with food—especially sticky or crumbly food.

Tips & Tricks from the Pros

I have a candy dish on my signing table. It draws people to you. Would work great with children's books. Make sure you have permission from the owner/manager first. Also, it's good to have a waste can for all the candy wrappers.

Bruce Raisch, author of *Ghost Towns of the Black Hills*, *Haunted Hotels of the West*, and other books.

Food can be a very effective selling tool if you have written a cookbook. The biggest cookbook event we've done at Red Lodge Books & Tea was for *Big Sky Cooking*, by Meredith Brokaw and Ellen Wright. My wife, Kathy, decided to have some fun with the event.

She went through the book, selected half a dozen recipes that would work for sampling, and spent the afternoon before the signing cooking them. She brought them all into the store and set them up along a counter, each with a sign saying something like, "Gingerbread with Whipped Cream, page 107."

She marked each of the foods she prepared—and several recipes she didn't make for the event—with a Post-it note in our personal copy of the book and set it on the counter for people to peruse.

After walking down the counter and sampling the foods, who could resist buying a copy of the cookbook? After the event, when Meredith and Ellen signed our book for us, they couldn't resist commenting on Kathy's Post-its.

big sky
cooking

MEREDITH BROKAW
AND ELLEN WRIGHT

PHOTOGRAPHS BY
TOM ECKERLE AND TOM MURPHY

for Kathy and Gary—
Keep the sticky notes and
cook away! Thank you
for hosting the book signing!
Meredith Brokaw
Ellen Wright

ARTISAN | NEW YORK

Copies of old books

My first book came out two decades ago. As a technical resource, it's been obsolete for a long time. There is still some good historical information in it and it has some fun stories from the old days, but nobody has shown any interest in actually buying a copy for close to ten years. I do, however, still have some.

Every now and then, when I'm addressing the right crowd, I'll take a copy of *The Court Reporters' Guide to Cyberspace* to an event and give it away. Sometimes we'll have a trivia contest, sometimes a random drawing. I always sign and personalize the book for the winner.

Copies of current books

Giving away copies of your new books is a different story. If your event is at a bookstore, every copy you give away for free

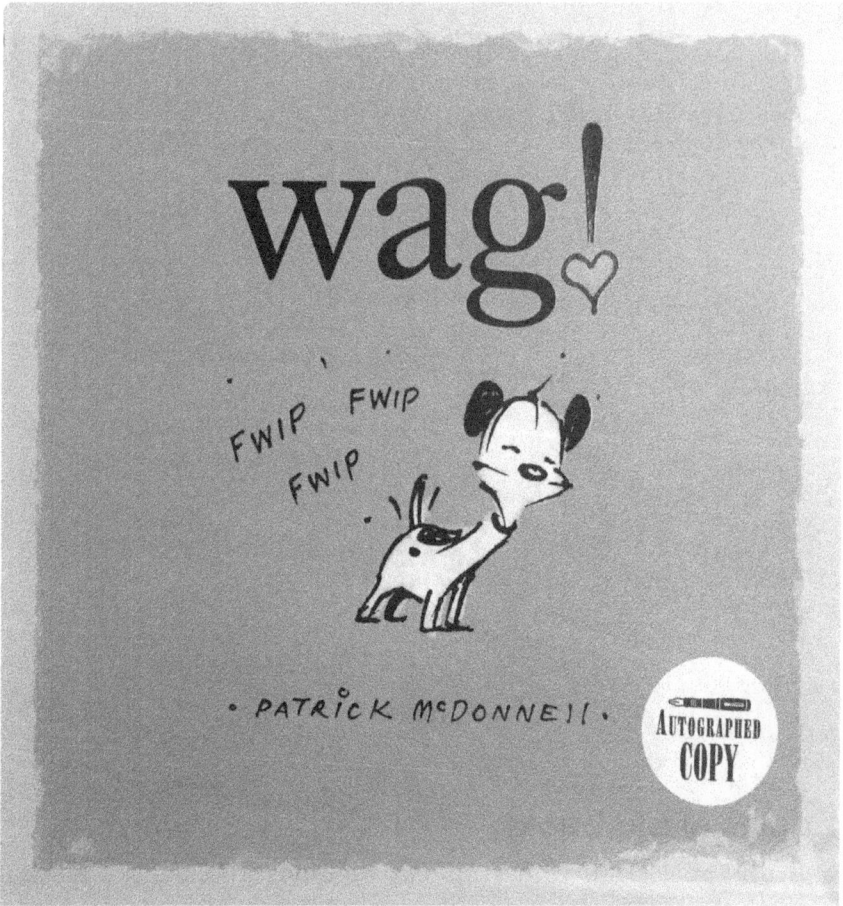

Putting on my bookstore owner hat for a moment, please let me offer you some book cover design advice: leave some empty space like Patrick McDonnell did here. Your book will sell better with a sticker that says it's autographed, but we don't want to have to cover your name with the sticker. With any luck, you'll also need room for a bestseller sticker!

takes away a sale from the store. You can do this at events where you do your own book sales, but not store events.

A much better idea is the package deal. Make arrangements with the store in advance, and then announce to customers that anyone who buys a copy of your new book gets a discount on your first book, or that your three books are $15 each, but you can buy all three for $40. You'll need to sell the books to the bookstore at a discount, of course, but it can be worth it.

Autographed copy stickers

Bookstores always keep rolls of stickers saying things like "autographed copy," "local author," or "bestseller." Other venues like gift shops typically don't. If you are signing stock after an event (which I recommend always doing), it's nice to have some stickers along to put on the covers. The picture on page 24 shows a fairly typical design.

Visual aids

Props add visual interest to your signing or talk. Did one of your characters find a Murex altispira shell on the beach? Put one on your signing table. Does your mystery hinge on a set of strange shell casings found at the scene of the murder? Bring along some bullets (or empty brass, if you're flying and you don't want to hassle with TSA about them). I've had authors bring along all kinds of interesting things, ranging from flowers to guns.

One of my favorites was when Bill Young was at my store with his mother Millicent signing copies of his book *Going for the Gold! The Journey with the WASP, Women's Airforce Service Pilots of World War II*. The only thing on the table other than the books and a sign was Millicent's Congressional Gold Medal. That's not something you get to see every day!

Millicent and Bill Young with Millicent's Congressional Gold Medal

Musicians that write books

When Daryl Brown, son of rhythm & blues legend James Brown, went on tour for his book *Inside the Godfather: Never Before Told Stories of James Brown by His Inner Circle*, he told a lot of stories about his father. He also talked about how he came to play guitar in James Brown's band (it's not the story you'd expect).

Daryl knows how to read an audience. When he looked around our tea bar, he didn't see a group of generic book fans; he saw music fans. He saw James Brown fans. One attendee brought along his copy of an early James Brown album. Daryl put the group at ease and told everybody he was happy to give a canned talk if they wanted it, but he was also happy to just answer questions and chat. And that's when he pulled out the best possible prop for his talk: his guitar.

Daryl Brown with his guitar at a book signing

He chatted with the crowd; he played a few tunes; he gave the attendees an evening to remember. Perhaps I'm biased when I talk about what a great prop the guitar was, but that's only because he let me play it!

Daryl isn't the only musician to write a book, nor is he the only one to play in our store. Jim Johnson, author of *Crossing the Bar*, brought along his guitar for a book signing and entranced the crowd with it.

Booksellers should be aware, though, that some musicians—especially former musicians—don't want to turn their book event into a concert. If you ask them about playing or singing in your store and they turn you down, don't push. Authors don't get paid for book signings, but musicians do get paid for performing. Respect their wishes.

Props you can sell

If there's something else you can sell in addition to your book, go for it, but make sure it's okay with the venue first. Most stores want all sales to go through their register, and if they don't have your items in their system, they could well say no.

I've taken along souvenir items like hats, and sold a few at events. In my experience, you're better off with a nice embroidered hat with your book title or logo on it, like these:

In some cases, you can make more from the "extra" items than you can from the books.

Dennis Linnehan is a photographer that put out a book called *Yellowstone and Grand Teton Splendor*. He called me before his signing and asked if it would be okay if he brought along some of his photographic prints to sell. I was okay with it, and the photos made his signing table more striking and attention-getting, even though he didn't sell a lot of prints at the event.

Note the key phrase in that last paragraph: "He called me before his signing and asked if it would be okay...."

The biggest darned prop I've ever seen

Craig Johnson created a fictional county for his protagonist, Sheriff Walt Longmire. When his mystery series was turned into a television series, they purchased a set of identical vehicles to use on set at Longmire's sheriff truck; apparently they wreck a lot of vehicles shooting that show. Johnson bought a matching one and asked for a set of duplicate decals.

When he showed up for his most recent reading and talk, he brought that vehicle along and parked it out in front.

As a side note if you're considering this trick yourself, even though Absaroka County doesn't really exist, driving around in this vehicle could be seen as impersonating a law enforcement officer, which most police departments take pretty seriously. Do what Craig did: use magnetic decals that are easy to put on for the event and remove when you're actually driving around.

Fans who may have missed the advertising for the event could still spot the sheriff truck parked in front of the event, and Craig was happy to take pictures with fans standing by the truck. That's him on the left with my wife and me.

Remember earlier when I was talking about having a "look"? Craig Johnson gets that. He's a Wyoming rancher writing books about a Wyoming sheriff, so he makes sure to look like it!

Yes, that's poop

Props are a highly effective way to start a conversation, and starting conversations sells books. Lest that sound entirely mercenary, I'm a social animal and I do love having conversations. But back to the main point…

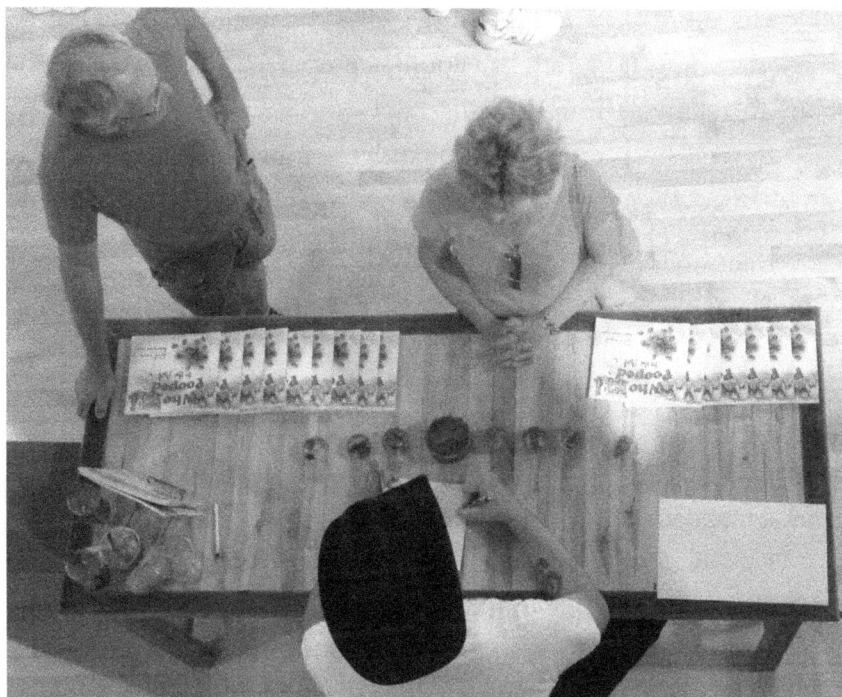

Balconies give people a unique perspective on book signing events.

In this picture, you can see a row of round things on the table in front of me. You can also see rows of books. Sometimes I do rows, sometimes big spiral stacks, sometimes pyramids. The round things on the table are samples of animal scat (a.k.a. "poop") that I have cast in resin. The big one in the middle is bear scat — always a crowd pleaser. That thing in the lower left is not poop. It's my lunch.

My poop samples are fabulous conversation starters. Each one has a label on the bottom stating what kind of animal it's from. I play guessing games with the kids, and sometimes with the grown-ups. They often have the effect of drawing people to the table. Sometimes they have the opposite effect, like when a little boy grabs one and runs at his mother, holding the sample in front of him and shouting "Look, Mom! It's real bear poop!"

His mom didn't come and visit my table, but I did rather enjoy watching how fast she could scamper backward across the lobby to get away from her son.

Even if I can't get someone quickly interested in the book, I can often get them interested in the poop samples. "Where did you get these?," they'll ask. "Are you sure this is from a red fox?" If your props are unusual, make sure you have a story for them.

I wanted to make sure that if I have a sample labeled as raccoon poop, then I'm totally, completely, 100% positive that it came from an honest-to-goodness raccoon. To accomplish that, I went to our local wildlife sanctuary and asked to collect scat samples from the animal enclosures.

For insurance purposes (and to keep crazy people away from their animals, I'm sure), they wouldn't let me go in with the animals, but one of the keepers volunteered to collect the samples for me. I took a handful of Ziploc bags and followed him from enclosure to enclosure. I carefully labeled a bag, and then he went in and collected the poop. If the poop was in the wolf pen, then I'm pretty darned sure it came out of one of the wolves.

PowerPoint presentations

Generally, I don't recommend slide shows for novelists. Your novel speaks for itself, and people are there to get a peek inside your head. Words are your business. Focus on those rather than creating images to back you up.

On the other hand, slide shows are great tools for nonfiction writers. Give your readers a glimpse of what's inside the book, and then extend it with more information and more pictures. If your book is printed in black & white, choose a few pictures that you wish you could have printed in color and include those in the presentation. You want people telling your friends, "the book was great, but you should have been at this event!"

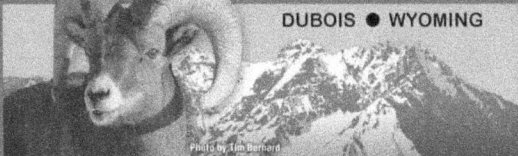

Who Pooped?
in the Park

Canyon Creek School
Billings, MT
April 2013

Kid's Guides to Scats and Tracks

by Gary D. Robson

These are the opening slides in a presentation I gave in two different venues. It was the same talk, but I changed the title slide for each audience to make them feel a bit more like it was just for them.

Who Pooped?
in the Park

Kid's Guides to Scats and Tracks
by Gary D. Robson

NATIONAL
Bighorn Sheep
CENTER
DUBOIS ● WYOMING

July
2012

Photo by Tim Bernard

If you've written a children's book, turn it into a slide show. If your publisher can give you high-resolution artwork, that's fantastic. If not, cut the pages out of a copy of your book so they'll lay flat, and scan them. You can always use those cut-up pages in a collage. If you're the illustrator, you can use signed pages as giveaways or prizes.

For that matter, if you're the illustrator—and you have retained rights to the original art—your original drawings and sketches are a great secondary source of income.

Children are more into being read to than adults, and if you have more than a handful in attendance, it's easier to have the pages projected on a screen or wall behind you than try to hold up a book so that everyone can see it.

I've used both PowerPoint and Prezi for my talks. I tend to prefer PowerPoint for showing a series of pictures or book pages, like when I'm reading to a group of children. Prezi is great when you're giving a "guided tour" of something. It has a sense of movement that works beautifully for following a timeline, a career, or a journey.

Even if you're giving the exact same presentation you've given a hundred times before, customize the title slide to include the name of the store or other venue (see illustrations on previous page).

During the presentation, focus on entertaining and informing the audience, not selling books. If they like you and enjoy your talk, the book sales will take care of themselves. That doesn't mean, of course, that you shouldn't close with a shameless plug. Heck, you can even *call* it a shameless plug.

And a Shameless Plug

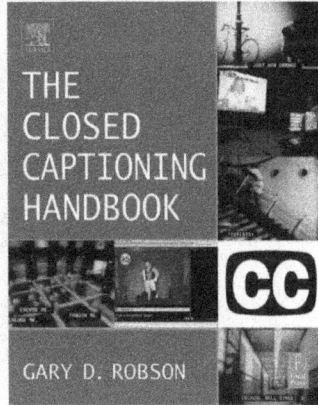

ALTERNATIVE REALTIME
CAREERS
A GUIDE TO CLOSED CAPTIONING AND
CART FOR COURT REPORTERS

BY GARY D. ROBSON

THE
CLOSED
CAPTIONING
HANDBOOK

GARY D. ROBSON

CC

June 2007   MCRA/Robson   59

The closing slide from a talk I did at a conference. I wanted to make sure everyone knew I'd be selling books in the back of the room after the talk.

This isn't really necessary if you're talking in a bookstore. People came with the understanding that you're an author and they know what books you wrote. But if you're speaking as an expert at a school, trade show, conference, or similar event, it's good to include a reminder at the end of what you have to offer.

A difficult question is how much contact information to include at the end. For me, this varies depending on the venue and the type of presentation. If I'm speaking to a group of booksellers at a book conference, I'll give them every possible way to get hold of me, including my cell phone number. If I'm speaking to a group of sixth-graders, I'll generally limit the contact info to very public information like my website and social media contacts.

Who Pooped?
in the Park

GaryDRobson.com
Facebook.com/WhoPooped
Twitter.com/GaryRobson

Kid's Guides to Scats and Tracks

by Gary D. Robson

Give out only the contact info you want that audience to have!

They could find all of this information on their own quite easily, but there's a reason to put it in the slide. I would rather have kids that read my books connect with the author page on Facebook that's set up for them than find my personal page. By including contact information, you increase the chances of them finding you where you want to be found, instead of doing an online search that produces your home phone number or personal email address.

The Launch Party

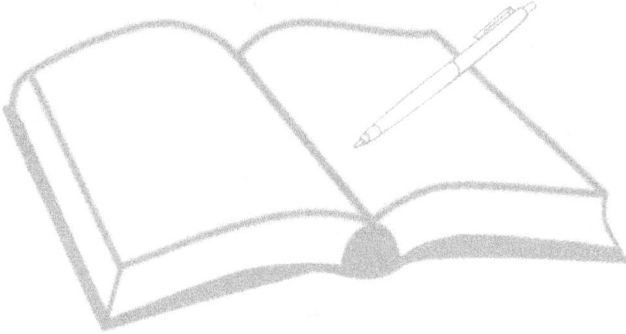

I f you are lucky enough to have a publicist, you can hand off a lot of your event planning and scheduling. Publicists are specialists in setting up book tours, and they can open doors for you that you might have trouble opening yourself. There's one event, though, that you need to take control of yourself, and that's the first one on the schedule.

Whether it's your first book or your fiftieth, a launch party is a great way to kick things off. Don't delegate this one to your publicist. It's too personal.

For most authors, the launch party will be the biggest single event they do, and it usually isn't part of a formal book tour. You may want to just make it a private party. Have a bunch of friends over to the house, put a pile of books on the kitchen table, and lay out the hors d'oeuvres and drinks. That kind of party can be a lot of fun, although you can end up doing a lot of work and spending a lot of money—not to mention dealing with people who show up expecting a free copy of your book.

Even if you do have a private party at your house, you should consider having a formal launch party at your friendly neighborhood bookstore or other retail outlet as well. Why?

- A bookstore will market the party to a larger crowd than you can probably reach. They keep email lists and have followers on social media, not to mention signs in the front window promoting events.
- You don't have to worry about selling the books and collecting the money. This is a huge advantage if you are one of those authors that feels uncomfortable asking people for money.
- Speaking of asking for money, people generally don't expect free books if the launch party is at a bookstore.
- You don't have to do much cleanup after the launch party, and people won't expect a lavish spread of free food and drinks.
- You're more likely to get media coverage when the event is held in a store or other public place.
- Your launch party can be festive even if it's held in a store. I have had launch parties in my store where the authors and their friends showed up with cakes, balloons, flower arrangements, and even a keg of beer.

The most important thing to keep in mind is that you may do a hundred book signings, but your book will only have one launch party. Get everything done well in advance so that when launch day arrives you can just relax and have fun with old friends and new, basking in the glow of your new book.

Tales from the Front Lines

When I published my book, my only book, in 2011, we were assured that I would receive a batch of 100 of them in plenty of time for my book-launch party, an affair to which I had invited a few hundred people.

I forget now exactly what caused the delay, but we found out two days before the launch that the books would not arrive for another three or four days. It was way too late to cancel the book launch, so when approximately 100 people showed up at the event, the first thing I had to do was to confess. I softened the blow by listing all the things we did have: beer and wine, excellent catered hors d'oeuvres and live music. The only thing we didn't have, ahem, were any books.

I said the best we could do was take orders that day, and I promised to mail them to anyone outside the Billings area and to hand-deliver them to everyone else. So there I sat, not signing books but taking orders and writing down addresses. It worked, more or less, but I still feel a pang of jealousy and regret when I go to a launch party and see the author, pen in hand, seated at a table between two enormous stacks of books. That could have been me!

Ed Kemmick, author of *The Big Sky, By and By: True Stories, Real People and Strange Times in the Heart of Montana*.

The timing of the launch

It is tempting to set up a launch party for the day your books will arrive. Your excitement and giddiness will be at their peak. It's a way to roll out the book with no sneak peaks and no spoilers. All in all, it's the perfect timing for a party.

Except for one thing.

As I write these words, cases of my latest book are on their way here for the launch event. Weeks ago, we carefully calculated the final schedule, determined when the books would arrive, and scheduled the party...for yesterday.

Yes, we advertised in the newspaper, made posters, set up a display at the bookstore, created a Facebook event, told everyone that came into the store, and generally did all of those things one does before a book launch. Unfortunately, there was a printing delay, and the books we expected several days ago still aren't here.

We rolled the dice on this one and lost. We took the gamble on purpose, because it is December, and we wanted people to buy the books as Christmas presents. We're taking pre-orders and we've rescheduled the party, but things would have worked out much better had we allowed an extra week, just in case.

The key to an event like this is communication, a theme you'll see repeated throughout this book. Let me provide examples of the right way and the wrong way to communicate on a launch party:

The right way

One of the most successful book launches my bookstore ever had was for a local author named Shirley McJunkin, who had written a memoir called *Homesteading on the Kenai*.

When we set things up, she asked if it would be okay to bring in a cake with her book cover on it. I said it certainly would. A while later, she stopped by and told me that she was concerned about space. A lot of her friends and family were planning to attend, and the bookstore wasn't very big back then. I made arrangements to move the party to the library — something I don't normally do because I want the people at the party to be able to browse the store, and possibly buy other books in addition to the new one.

Because Shirley kept us up-to-speed on everything that was happening and brought extra books on her own to cover the crowd, we had an outstanding event and sold sixty books, which is a big number for a self-published debut author in a small town. One of her friends brought a flower arrangement, another brought a big coffee pot, and a third brought a cooler full of lemonade. The launch party really did feel like a party, and the pictures in the newspaper after the event helped to fuel future sales of the book.

Everybody won.

The wrong way

I won't name any names in this tale. When I first spoke with this author about his upcoming book, we made plans for a pretty big event. The book was being very well publicized, so I got ready for a capacity crowd (this event was years after the Shirley McJunkin party, and we'd expanded the store since then). We arranged the signing after hours, cleared furniture out of the way, and ordered a lot of books.

Sometimes authors don't realize that "returnable" books can still cost a bookstore a lot of money. When ordering from a big distributor like Ingram or Baker & Taylor, the store receives a discount of about 40%. If we return books, we pay freight to send them back, and our account is credited at 50% of the cover price. On a $30 hardback book, it can cost the store $4 for each book returned. If a store were to buy 40 of those $30 books, sell 10, and return the other 30, they would make $120 on the books they sold, and lose $120 on the ones they returned, and that's after all of the time and money spent on advertising and promotion.

Authors also don't always realize why it's important to keep the bookstore up to speed on things happening outside the store. This particular author set up a launch party at his home a couple of nights before the launch party at the store. Had we known about this in advance, it wouldn't have been a problem. We would have ordered fewer books and planned for a smaller event.

As it was, most of the author's friends and family bought books from him at the private party and didn't attend the launch party in our store. We were stuck with cases of books and ended up losing money on the event.

The author thought I was upset because he had done his own party and cut me out of some book sales. In reality, I didn't care whether he had his own party; I just wanted to know about it in advance so I could plan accordingly.

Setting Up Events

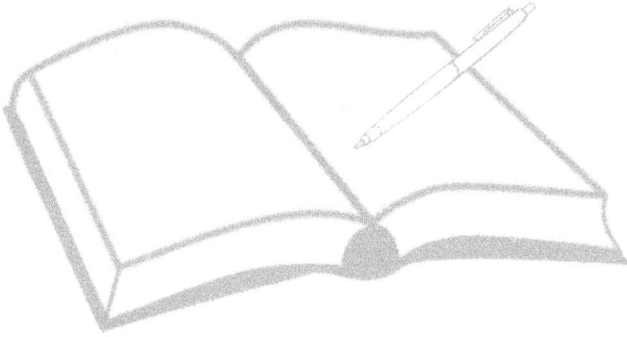

When I say "book signing," what image pops into your head? An author parked behind a table with a line of people waiting to buy books? That's the image most people have. They figure a signing will give them a very short interaction with the author: a few sentences exchanged at most.

A "book event," on the other hand, could be anything from a formal reading or slide show to a group of people sitting around and informally chatting with an author.

The exact wording for the event announcements can vary. Try different ideas to see what works best for you. You don't have to stay with generic phrases like "meet the author" or "book talk," either. When I do events for my children's series about animal poop and tracks called *Who Pooped in the Park?* I use titles like "Get the straight poop with Gary Robson" or "Meet Gary Robson and find out Who Pooped."

Where to stay

If you are looking for a place to stay in an unfamiliar town, the best person to ask is a local, and the bookstore hosting your event is filled with helpful locals. Ask them for recommendations, as they know their town a lot better than you do. If you're lucky, you can sign at a place like BookBar in Denver, which has a bed & breakfast (called "BookBed," of course) right upstairs from the store.

There are authors that couch surf their way through a book tour, crashing at the homes of friends and acquaintances in each town they visit. This is a great way to keep costs down, but if you're going to discuss it with the bookstore owners or event coordinators, broach the subject delicately.

Tell the store owner that you're traveling on a tight budget and ask for an inexpensive place to spend the night. That may get you an invitation to stay at their place. Don't just say, "I'd love to do a book signing at your store if I can sleep at your house that night." That may shut down the whole event.

Finding bookstores

So you've decided to take your show on the road. You've put together a list of places where you think your book will sell well, but you haven't been to all of those towns. How do you find the right store to host your signing?

I recommend starting with the American Booksellers Association. Go to their website, bookweb.org, and pull up the member directory. This will give you a list of independent bookstores in that area. At the bottom of each page on the ABA's site is a list of nine regional trade associations as well. Some stores may join their regional association without joining the national association, so check both.

To continue building your list, you can use Google, contact other authors, and check websites for chains like Barnes & Noble. Wherever possible, find the names of the people who handle events at each store and contact them directly.

The best way to set up an event at a bookstore is through personal contact. If you can stop by the store with a copy of your book in hand, do it. If not, make a phone call, but keep it brief and make sure you have information ready to email on a moment's notice, including a quick synopsis, a picture of the cover, purchasing information, and a link to an excerpt.

When dealing with bookstore owners, managers, and buyers, stay positive. Be persistent, but never pushy. If you can take "no" gracefully, the door is still open to go back in later. If you get angry or argue with the store owner or buyer, you will never get back in.

Working with a publicist

Earlier this year, I had a comical exchange of emails concerning a book signing. The author and the publicist contacted me separately, trying to schedule the same event on different dates.

It was very confusing at first, until I realized that the author and the publicist had never talked to each other. They were both setting up the book tour, hitting different towns on a different schedule. Each got annoyed at me for talking to the other, so I finally gave up and told them both to leave my store out of their plans.

You can avoid this kind of fiasco by working out a plan with the publicist before starting to make phone calls and visits. Also, if the publicist is in charge of setting up the tour, make sure to cc the publicist on every single email you send to an event host.

Tell your publicist to email you immediately after setting up a new event. Check each one to make sure the schedule works for you.

I had a Wyoming author scheduled for an event at my bookstore. I had met the author at a conference, and he put me in touch with his publicist at one of the big New York City publishing houses to work out the details of a Saturday signing.

The day before the event, the author called me, and opened the conversation by saying, "My publicist is an idiot."

It turned out that the publicist had scheduled him for a signing in Yellowstone Park in the morning and my store in the afternoon. It made sense to the publicist. It says right on my store's website that we're about 65 miles from Yellowstone, so he figured he was perfectly safe allowing a couple of hours of driving time. The problem is that we're 65 miles from the northeast entrance to the park—over an 11,000 foot mountain pass—and his signing was near the southwest corner. It's a five-hour trip.

We had to reschedule the signing at the last minute, changing it from a Saturday to a Monday afternoon. Not only do daytime events on weekdays have very little draw, but it was too late for updated newspaper ads. We ended up selling one book.

No matter who makes the initial contact with the store, make sure they have a way to get hold of you directly. If an emergency comes up, they might not be able to track down your publicist after hours.

It's also good practice to call the store a few days in advance to confirm everything.

Doing events with a co-author

Again, communication is paramount. Make sure you're not stepping on each other's feet when setting up the events. Work out who is responsible for what before you start contacting stores.

When you do start contacting event hosts, make sure they understand that you're both coming. Most stores hosting a book signing event will assume that they need room for one person. A single table, a single chair. If you are bringing along a photographer, illustrator, co-author, editor, or other accomplice, make sure to let them know in advance so they can allow space for that second person!

What can you expect?

As the anecdotes throughout this book will demonstrate, nobody can predict how a book event will go. If you aren't a well-known author in a busy location, selling five or ten books is a pretty typical signing.

Sometimes, the book gods (I think their names are Alexandria and Gutenberg) smile upon you. You have the right book at the right location at the right time, and you walk away exhausted but exhilarated, leaving behind a pile of empty book boxes and a cash register full of money.

Other times, your table is behind the Sanskrit dictionaries, the bookstore cat piddles on your new shoes, and the only person that talks to you the whole time is the 19-year-old store manager making a pity purchase for his collection of signed books that he will eventually give to the local homeless shelter or sell on eBay.

If you pay attention, you'll learn something from each event you do. The good events will get better, and the bad ones won't be quite so horrific.

Non-traditional venues

As I mentioned in the introduction, I have signed books in a whole lot of interesting places. You need to consider the venue that fits your book the best when you're planning events.

I always try to schedule my book signings and talks in an independent bookstore when I can, because I feel that indie stores and second or third-tier authors like me have a symbiotic relationship (I suppose that symbiosis got a little out of hand when I bought a bookstore, but that's another subject entirely). The more we support each other, the better we both do.

That said, there are times when a bookstore just isn't the best place to promote your book. When I'm giving a talk to promote *The Closed Captioning Handbook*—my book about television technology that provides accessibility for deaf and hard-of-hearing people—I plan on a tech conference or a college campus. I don't think anybody has ever bought a copy of that book in an indie bookstore.

Signing books in a warehouse

John Clayton writes about the people and places of the American West. His book, *The Cowboy Girl: The Life of Caroline Lockhart* (a finalist for the High Plains Book Award), and his upcoming history of Yellowstone National Park are tailor-made for indie bookstore events. His publisher decided another of John's books, *Stories from Montana's Enduring Frontier*, would be just right in Costco. After that event, he wrote a guest post on David Abrams' "Quivering Pen" book blog, which John graciously allowed me to reprint here in its entirety (see "Tales from the Front Lines" on page 50).

Signing at the Yellowstone Wildlife Sanctuary

In our town, there is a wildlife sanctuary. Each year, they hold various fund-raisers and community outreach events. In 2009, they asked if I would come and give a talk about animal scat, and perhaps even read from one of my *Who Pooped in the Park?* books.

I was happy to do it. They set up a big open house day, with barbecued burgers and hotdogs (I'm fairly certain we didn't eat any former residents of the sanctuary), tours, activities, and education stations. They set me up on the lawn by the barbecues, because everyone wants to hear about animal droppings while enjoying a fresh-cooked burger.

I worried for a bit when clouds moved in overhead. I hadn't prepared for rain. My trademark cowboy hat would help to keep the rain off me, but I had no way to protect my books, and I didn't think too many people would hang around and listen to me in the rain. After a while, though, the clouds dispersed and with them, my worries, although I do plan for rain now when doing outdoor events.

When I started to talk, a modest crowd accumulated. The smaller kids sat cross-legged on the lawn, the parents stood behind them, and the teenagers leaned against trees with bored expressions on their faces as I talked about excrement. No worries. The teenagers aren't my target audience anyway.

I chatted about fox feces, moose manure, and deer dung until I noticed that most of the little children weren't looking at me. They were looking past me, and whispering excitedly to each other. I turned and looked.

A tiny little rabbit had hopped out from the underbrush and was sitting only a few yards away from me. The only thing that could have made the moment more memorable would have been if it had pooped on cue. Maybe I need to start taking a bunny with me when I do outdoor events. He sure did liven things up.

When I told other authors that I was about to do a book signing at Costco in Billings, Montana, the reaction was curiosity, jealousy, horror, or all three. So what's it like to be a non-famous author doing a book event at a warehouse store?

Everything ran incredibly smoothly. The event was set up by my publisher, The History Press, and Costco's book distributor, American West Books. Advance emails reminded everyone of their responsibilities. The store set up an attractive display table on the main traffic corridor. All I had to do was show up.

In general, I prefer to do a "reading" or "lecture" or "discussion" rather than a "signing." Even if very few people show up for a lecture, at least we have a structure in which to discuss literature. By contrast, a signing involves long periods of feeling weirdly "on display," interrupted by episodes of partially-faked informality that reside in a netherworld between cocktail party and commerce. Before I'd done any signings myself, as a customer I tended to avoid signing tables for unfamiliar authors, worried that "meeting the author" would obligate me to buy the book. (Later, I realized the author is, or should be, delighted for any conversation, and the perfect exit line is, "Good luck with your book.")

The signing did have two drawbacks. First, I felt bad about participating in an event that would compete with independent bookstores. Like many authors and readers, I treasure independent bookstores and want to give them advantages such as personal author appearances. I would not do a Costco event in Bozeman or Missoula, where I have favorite independents. But in Billings, a Barnes & Noble is the only new-bookstore within fifty miles of Costco. This may be a weak self-justification, since Costco draws customers from more than fifty miles away, but it was further enhanced by the fact that I was simply following the wishes of my publisher, which (one would hope) should know more about bookselling than I do.

The second drawback was that the book was selling at a thirty-five percent discount. This not only increased the potential competition with other bookselling outlets, but also decreased my royalties by thirty-five percent. On its own, the event didn't even pay for the gas to get there, much less my time. Of course, the cost/benefit problem extends to many types of book events, with justifications including improved area media coverage (though Costco did no such outreach), improved retailer relations (other Costcos are also carrying the book), and the chance for growing word-of-mouth sales.

But the Costco setting minimizes the drawbacks of a signing, in two ways. First, there are just so many people in the store, especially on a Saturday at noon. This was especially true for me doing an event at my local Costco: I bided my time chatting with some friends who just happened to be replenishing their pantries. And although many, many people passed by without even noticing me—because few people go to Costco to buy books—at least I had an ideal seat from which to do great people-watching.

Second, the Costco tradition of giving away "free samples" has familiarized its customers with the notion of engaging with a product demonstrator regardless of intention to buy. Inspired by the wonderful author Jess Walter's story of giving away his own "free samples," I decided I too would cut up my page-proofs into sentence-sized fragments for the giveaway.

I toyed with going fully ironic, doing the samples as a mocking gesture—perhaps I would wear a hairnet, or mumble "fat-free and low in sodium" as customers walked past. But as soon as I arrived, I realized two things: first, I felt an incredible solidarity with the other product demonstrators. (One even bought the book.) Second, even had I wanted to mock them (or at least the situation they found themselves in), the audience at a Costco on a Saturday noon is not really interested in self-ironic performance art. The gesture would have been lost.

On the other hand, "free samples" did prove a surprisingly effective sales tool. For example, one customer said, "Well, this sample mentions the Bighorn mountains, which are my favorite, so I guess I need to buy a copy." I'm now tempted to do free samples even at non-Costco events.

Oh, and one more factor, at least when it comes to "my first...": when I learned about the event, I googled "Costco book signing" to see if someone could prepare me for what it would be like. I didn't find much. So I hope publishing this essay will help others, and bring David and me some positive karma.

John Clayton, author of *The Cowboy Girl* and *Stories From Montana's Enduring Frontier* (www.JohnClaytonBooks.com).

Actually, that isn't the only time I had an unexpected companion at a book event. In 2005, I was signing in a general store in Yellowstone, and they had placed me directly in front of the main entrance with a huge stone fireplace as a backdrop. Perfect location! Everyone who came in saw my table.

My wife and son had come along, but since I was scheduled to sit there for several hours, they wandered off. When they returned, my son, Doug, asked about the toy bat on the fireplace next to me.

As it turns out, it wasn't a toy. It was a real, live little brown bat who had been hanging there a few feet away from me for the whole event.

Tips & Tricks from the Pros

Serendipitous animal companions like my bat buddy in Yellowstone are fine, but always *always* check with the venue before bringing your own animal along. We've had several animal-centered events in my store, including owls and rats at Harry Potter parties and a hugely popular signing event for a book about therapy dogs. The author brought along a Saint Bernard and a giant ink pad. The author personalized each book that was purchased and then pressed the dog's foot on the ink pad and put a paw print on the title page.

This worked beautifully in our dog-friendly store, but other store owners might not have looked so kindly upon an author showing up with a 200 pound dog. The owner presented the paw print idea in our initial conversation and made it part of the plan from the beginning. That's the right way to do it!

Gary D. Robson

Before the Signing

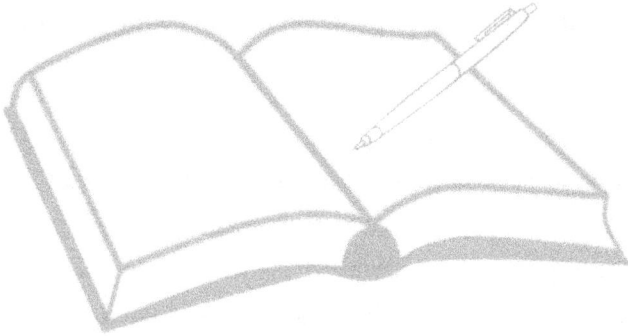

CHAPTER 5

The number one requirement for a successful book signing is communication. If you have to leave at 6:00, tell them that in advance. If you'd like to go out and have a beer with the store owner after the event, don't wait until the day of the signing to ask. Tell them whether you're bringing books and what you'll charge the store for them. If you need to be paid for books on the spot, say so. There may not be anyone there with check signing authority when the signing finishes up.

Communication by itself is not enough, though. You need to arrive at the signing ready to go. Some of your prep work can take place a few minutes before you leave for the event, but some needs to be done well in advance.

Pack your signing kit

Whether you carry a box, backpack, or briefcase, there are certain items you always want to have along when you do a book signing event. The more signings you do, the more you'll refine your kit. Here's what I take along, in addition to the signage and props from the previous chapter:

Camera

This has become easier as the quality of cell phone cameras has increased. There's no longer any need to bring along a bulky SLR camera just to get some pictures of the event for your blog, scrapbook, or social media.

Pen(s)

Bring a spare pen in case you run out of ink. Make sure that you either choose pens with quick-drying ink or bring along blotter paper. Customers won't be happy if they buy your book and the signature turns out to be a big black smear because they closed the book before the ink was dry on the signature.

Pad for writing names

Also bring a little notepad or Post-it pad where people can write down the spellings of their names. This is more critical than it's ever been because of the plethora of spellings, even on common names.

There have always been numerous ways to spell Kathryn/Catherine, but I'm seeing news ways of spelling old names all the time. At one signing, I was asked to sign a book to Don & Sue. Luckily, I asked the spellings, because it was actually going to Donn & Soo.

When things aren't busy, you can just ask and let people spell the names to you. When you start to develop a line—or if you have trouble with accents—it becomes faster and safer to have them write the names down for you. At a really packed signing, you'll want someone walking down the line with a pad getting the names written down in advance.

Business cards

A writer has two reasons to carry business cards: to give fans and to give professional contacts in the book business. Those two reasons are very different. So different, in fact, that I'd recommend making up two different sets of cards—or using business cards for professional contacts and bookmarks for fans (see previous chapter).

When you're handing a card to a staff member in a bookstore or other people in the trade such as editors, agents, or other authors, you want them to be able to get hold of you directly. That card should have information that will remind them of who you are (e.g., name, website, social media handles, and book titles) just as the cards for fans should. But professional cards also need to have your phone number, email address, and possibly mailing address—information you don't want to hand out to random fans.

Bookplates

From time to time you'll encounter people that say, "I wish I'd known you were going to be here. I'd have brought my copies of your books to sign." If you pick up a few packages of bookplates (stickers that go in the front of the book), you can sign a bookplate for them instead of letting them leave empty-handed.

For most authors, generic bookplates work fine. If you want to stand out from the crowd, have a roll of custom stickers printed for you, or buy sheets of blank stickers and print them yourself.

It's also good to have bookplates if the store runs out of books at the signing. You really don't want the fans to leave empty-handed.

Your own personal copy of your book for reading

Do not take a new book from the bookstore's stock, crease the pages, and read from it during your talk (yes, I've actually seen someone do this). Instead, have a copy of your own with bookmarks, notes, sticky tabs, and whatever else you might need in it. Your reading will look much more professional if you can flip the book directly open to the passage(s) you plan to read. If you have a great story that goes with one of those passages, note it in the book so you don't forget about it.

A brief biography in large print

If you're giving a talk, especially in a larger store, a member of the staff will probably introduce you to the crowd. Most of the time, this will be a staff member that has either read the book or done a bit of research about you. Just in case, though, have a short introduction written out ahead of time that you can just hand someone—and make sure it's printed in a large enough font that the staff member doesn't have to run and find their glasses to read it.

If someone in the store has done their homework and prepared an introduction, don't be offended if they use that one instead of the one you brought. If I'm introducing well known authors that have been to town several times, I may tell a quick story about their previous visits instead of using a formal introduction.

A sign-up sheet for your newsletter

If you have an email newsletter, subscriptions are gold! The more people voluntarily opt in to your mailing list, the broader the audience you have when you announce your next book or special event. Print up some forms and leave them out on your table so that people can join your list. Make sure the form mentions how often you send out newsletters; people may be happy to subscribe to a monthly email, but hesitant to add their name to a daily list.

Always thank them for adding their name, but don't get pushy. We all get too much email as it is, and some people just don't want to add any more.

Gary D. Robson

A thermos or water bottle

If the store doesn't have a coffee shop or tea bar, bring a bottle of water or thermos of hot drink with you (save the booze for after the book signing, please).

You probably think I'm kidding with that last parenthetical, don't you? One of the authors who supplied tips & tricks for this book actually included "don't show up drunk" as their first tip. The author later called me and said, "don't use that one."

Communication with the venue

Who's bringing books (and how many?)

In 2011, I was asked to give a talk at the Grizzly & Wolf Discovery Center in West Yellowstone, Montana. I was scheduled to talk in their theater from 7:00 to 8:00 p.m., and then sign books in their gift shop afterward. I publicized the talk and signing on Facebook, Twitter, and my blog, leaving the local publicity to the Grizzly & Wolf Center — and I made sure the West Yellowstone Chamber of Commerce knew about it. I sent them some artwork for posters and packed my big sign. Since they told me that they regularly carried *Who Pooped in the Park?* and it sold well, I assumed they'd have plenty of stock, but I tossed a few extras in the car, just in case.

See the problems? Hint: they're both in that last sentence, and there are two key words in each problem. The first one is "I assumed" and the second one is "a few." When I showed up a couple of hours early to check in and chat with the staff, one of the first things the manager said to me was, "we sold out of your books, so I hope you have plenty of them out in the car!" Oops. I had five. Count 'em, five.

Better communication could have prevented this from happening. As it was, we had to scramble.

Luckily, West Yellowstone is a small, friendly town. The gift shop manager at the Grizzly & Wolf Center knows the owner of the bookstore in town, and called her. Oops again. They were out of stock, too. Fortunately for us, a very pleasant assistant manager at another store in town (thank you, Smith & Chandler) had a big stack of books they were willing to share.

Talking poop in West Yellowstone

So all went well. I gave my talk to a good-sized group, and there were plenty of books for the signing. I also learned my lesson. I should have carried more books with me and I should have called the store before I left home to ask whether they would need books. Calling ahead might not have been adequate, though. My event was on a Sunday, and they had a good stock going into the weekend. She might have told me they had it covered, but it still would have been good to ask.

Gary D. Robson

I took all of the books that didn't sell back to Smith & Chandler in the morning and signed them all. The Grizzly & Wolf Center replaced the ones we sold that night when their next shipment came in later in the week. Everybody won.

If you have a series, have the first book there

Often, we'll have authors show up to sign their third — or twenty-third — book in a series. One of the first questions we get from attendees unfamiliar with the author is, "do I have to read the series in order?"

Have an answer ready for that question!

It does present a bit of a dilemma. If you say "yes," that may cost you a sale of your brand-new book: the hardback that gives you a higher royalty (which is also the one the publisher is watching to see if you get another contract). But if you say "no," you have a chance of selling your newest book and the first in the series.

In both cases, though, you want to have a few copies of that first book sitting on the table, just in case.

At this 2015 book signing by Keith McCafferty, the first book in his series was also the first book to sell out. The cookies probably helped!

If the store is buying from you, what are the terms?

If you want to avoid potential hard feelings after the event, this is an important detail to work out in advance.

Bookstores buy the majority of their books at a 40% discount off of the cover price. If you have a $15 book, they expect to pay $9 for it. Purchasing directly from the publisher often gets better discounts, typically in the 44% to 48% range, depending on the size of the order.

Offering a better discount means you have a chance of selling more books. A line like, "If you'd like more books for stock, I can offer you a 50% discount and since I have them right here, there's no shipping cost," has an excellent chance of leaving more of your books on the shelf when the event is over.

Offering a lower discount means that they're unlikely to buy books from you. Telling a store you can provide them with books at a 20% discount is like wearing a sign that says, "I'm new to this whole book thing."

In addition to the discount, make sure to discuss payment terms. There's not always someone at the store that can sign checks, and very few stores will pay in cash, so if you're expecting to walk out after the event with money in your pocket, it needs to be negotiated in advance.

Either carry an invoice book with you or pre-print some custom invoice sheets and take them along. You can buy invoice books at any office supply store, and either write in your name and contact information or use a stamp. Make sure they know who to make the check out to, where to mail it, and how soon you expect it.

Custom invoice sheets are an excellent alternative. They look professional, and if you design them right they are easy to fill out.

Harold "Muskie" Wilson

1234 Ondatra Way • Altoona, WI 54720
715-555-1212

ISBN	BOOK TITLE	QUANTITY	WHOLESALE	TOTAL
978-0000000-14-1	The Breeding Habits of Muskrats		$ 12.00	$
978-0000000-22-7	Murder Most Musky		$ 9.00	$
978-0000000-19-3	Hannibal's Elephants and Tennille's Muskrats		$ 12.00	$
978-0000000-31-X	The Complete Muskrat		$ 48.00	$
			Grand Total	$

Please make checks payable to Muskie Wilson Books

With this form, you only need to fill in the quantities, multiply each line, and total the form. It helps to either have a calculator along with you or learn how to use the one that probably came with your phone.

I'll swap you six books for a calendar and a stuffed bear

Other store owners may have different policies, but I don't barter. If you spot some books or tea in my store that you like, it makes lots of sense for both of us to just swap some of your stuff for some of my stuff. But that throws off my accounting and record keeping. I really do need to write you a check for your books and then run your purchase through my point-of-sale system.

In fact, I mentioned this earlier, but it bears repeating: If you need to be paid that day for any books that you've brought to the signing, tell the store personnel up front. Otherwise you may end up at the end of the event looking for money when the only person authorized to pay you has already left for the day.

Let the store know about special needs early

Do you need a second chair at the signing table for your spouse or assistant? Do you need a projector, screen, or computer for your talk? Do you need a power plug for an electronic picture frame or tablet? Do you use a wheelchair and need help setting up? Do you need an easel for your signs or an extra table for props? Do you need an Internet connection for a Prezi?

Figure it all out and tell the bookstore—preferably in writing (email or letter).

Do what you have to do beforehand

Booksellers don't like telling customers, "Yes, the book signing was supposed to start now, but the author is having a smoke/ going to the bathroom/buying a soda/calling home." Take care of everything in advance and be at your table or lectern ready to go a few minutes before the scheduled start time for the event.

Check in a bit early

As a bookseller, it frustrates me when an author is coming in from another state, and five minutes before the signing starts, I have no idea whether they're a block away or caught in traffic in another town. If you're running late, call and tell them. As my father always used to tell me, "If you're not five minutes early, you're late!" When you arrive, drop by the store and tell them you made it. Then (if you have time) go out and grab some dinner or do whatever else you have to do.

Showing up early can also help to deal with other potential problems. Most of the time, shops have a specific place set aside for signings, but if you let them know early enough, they may be able to accommodate special requests.

I had one author come into my store on a bright sunny day and comment that there were a lot of people on the street, but not many people inside. He said if I put his table out on the sidewalk, he could engage people as they walked by. Why not? I went ahead and moved his table. I'm not sure if we sold more books, but I had a very happy author sitting out in the sun and I got a lot of positive comments about him.

If a line forms, have someone (a bookstore worker or someone you have brought along) walk through the line with yellow sticky notes (3x3 inch preferred) and legibly write out the name they want the author to address the book to and any special words requested. This saves lots of time and prevents spelling errors as to the name.

Lynn Boughey, author of *Harry Potter and the Art of Spying* and *Mission to Chara.*

Bring spare books

If you're lucky, the signing will be a smash hit. With the economy down, though, booksellers are being cautious about over-ordering. That means that if your signing is fantastic, they just might run out of books. If you have a box or two in your trunk, you can grab them (be prepared to sell them to the store at the standard distribution discount) and keep on going. If you don't, the signing is done.

Don't bring those books in without asking first. You want it to be very clear which books are yours and which ones belong to the store. They may not be set up to buy from you, or it may take a manager to authorize bringing in outside books.

Don't bring in books that the store doesn't sell

If you've written more than one book, you want everybody to buy all of your books, right? While you should certainly carry around some extra copies of your other books, don't bring them in or push them until you've talked to the store management about them.

I found this out when I was signing books in Grand Teton National Park. I talked with a customer about my Sonoran Desert book (which I happened to have copies of in the car), but there was no way to sell one. The gift shop didn't have the Sonoran book in their computer, and it's tacky to drag the customer out in the parking lot to do a cash transaction out of the trunk of your car when you're in the middle of a book signing.

If you have more than one book, talk to the store in advance so you don't end up caught by surprise when this happens.

Work out the procedure

The store has final say over the flow of the event. They know their space and their customers, and they may have other special considerations you aren't aware of. It's fine to make requests or suggestions, but if they tell you how it's going to work, accept it gracefully.

Buy and then sign, or the other way around?

First, ask whether customers are expected to purchase the book before or after you sign it. There are advantages to both approaches.

People tend to feel a bit more rushed in the beginning. They want to hurry up and get in line, to make sure they get a book and make sure there's time for you to sign it. They also don't want to carry an armload of other books up to the signing table. After the book is signed, they'll be more relaxed and more likely to wander the store and buy more books. Many customers are reluctant to stand in line at the cash register more than once. If they can pay for the book after they have it signed, they are likely to spend more money in the store that day.

There are also risks associated with paying afterward. People may walk out with your book or realize that they didn't have enough money and leave behind a book that can't be sold to anyone else—although I did end up with a book after a signing once that the author had signed to someone who had the same first name as one of my family members. Christmas gift! It doesn't always work out, but it did that time.

In my store, I generally don't have people pay for the book before they have it signed unless it's a huge event.

What if customers bring in books to be signed?

Again, the store is going to make the final call on this, but I prefer to let customers bring in books from home. Few people actually do it, and the goodwill generated by letting them get their old books signed outweighs the potential for lost sales.

Most of the time, when someone brings in a book that wasn't purchased that day, it's an older copy or a first edition that they want signed. They wouldn't have purchased another anyway, so the store doesn't lose anything by letting them get it signed.

There's always someone rude enough to buy a book on Amazon and bring it into a bookstore to have it signed, but it's best to just sigh and ignore it. Making a fuss won't change a thing.

Tips & Tricks From the Pros

I have one gem of wisdom. Expect nothing, be grateful for everything, and collect stories of humiliation as if they were four leaf clovers. I've always thought that the real transaction in book signings was between author and bookseller (booksellers are gods). If I leave some fairy dust behind with a bookseller, it counts for a lot more (in sales) and in future friendships than bonding temporarily with a reader. I'm grateful for readers, grateful that anyone comes out for a reading or signing, but I've had signings with only three people (or less) that have been very successful because they were the beginning of a long-term relationship with the bookseller.

James W. Hall, author of *Hot Damn!* and the Thorn mysteries.

Tales from the Front Lines

As for my most memorable reading, it was while I was touring with *You Saved Me, Too*, my memoir on my friendship with a holocaust survivor. There was an old man in the audience who kept asking detailed questions about where my friend, Aron, had been imprisoned. Then he asked what Aron's tattoo number was. After I told him, the man raised his sleeve and showed me his. It only differed by a few digits, meaning he had been standing just a couple of men away from Aron back in 1943 in Auschwitz as the Nazi's marked them. The man in the audience didn't remember meeting Aron, but I'm sure they crossed paths. The fact that they had been so close and both survived was quite moving. I couldn't concentrate for the rest of the Q&A session because I was so excited to talk privately to the man.

Susan Kushner Resnick, author of *You Saved Me, Too: What a Holocaust Survivor Taught Me about Living, Dying, Fighting, Loving, and Swearing in Yiddish.*

Reading or Talking?

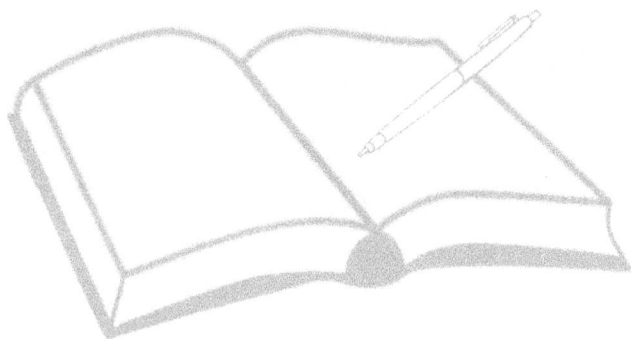

CHAPTER 6

You've done your prep. You've practiced the talk and decided which parts of the book you're going to read. If you're using a slide show, it is loaded, the projector is on, and the title slide is showing on the screen. The audience is seated, and it's time to make things happen.

I love this moment. Every presentation is a new experience, even if you've given the same talk dozens of time before. This is a different audience, a different venue, a different day. You're standing with one foot in the familiar and the other in the unknown, because this talk could go anywhere.

I learn something new every time I give a talk. That, actually, is one of the things I like most about public speaking: if I do it right, I learn as much as my audience does.

Obviously, it's the author's job to give a good talk, but the bookstore (or other venue) can provide a lot of help to make things go well.

Tips & Tricks for Booksellers

1. Build the author up in your introduction. If his or her book received a starred review from *Publisher's Weekly* or whatever, mention it. This gives the author confidence and negates the need for him to blow his own horn. Authors, even established authors, can be very insecure.

2. Ask the first question when it's time for questions. And the second if need be to break the ice.

3. Restrict the actual reading time to five to fifteen minutes, tops. People in the audience are generally much more interested in hearing the writer speak than hearing him read. One of the most successful bookstore owners I know, Barbara Peters at the Poisoned Pen, forbids authors to read anything at all.

4. Emphasize questions at the event. Most authors are more interesting and relaxed answering questions than they are giving a presentation. This is true not only of new and nervous authors but of established authors who have given the same presentation time and time again. It is refreshing for them to answer questions and they come across as more spontaneous and genuine.

Keith McCafferty, award-winning author of *Crazy Mountain Kiss* and the rest of the Sean Stranahan series.

Gary D. Robson

Talk about the book

No matter whether you're there for a simple book signing, a reading, or some other kind of talk, the main reason people have come to the event is to hear about your book.

I generally agree with Keith McCafferty's second tip (talk, don't read), with one exception: children's picture books. Little kids love to be read to, and they would much rather hear you read your book than listen to you talk about why and how you wrote it.

Let's make that two exceptions: poets often read their own work with a rhythm and expressiveness that readers might not pick up from the printed page.

Here's another author's take on reading vs. speaking:

Tips & Tricks From the Pros

I have two don'ts and one do—at least that work for us.

1. Don't read from your book unless you are a Nobel Laureate. Let your readers do the reading.

2. Don't lecture—entertain.

3. Don't try to sell your book and don't try to summarize it. Tell stories about how you came to write it instead.

Douglas Preston, author of dozens of books, including the bestselling Pendergast series with Lincoln Child.

In Preston's second tip, "entertain" does not mean you should try to be a stand-up comedian, unless your book is a comedy and you are really good at stand-up. It means you should make the presentation interesting.

Always find a way to start off with a locally-focused comment. Mention your previous trip to that bookstore. Talk about a great experience you had in that town. You can even talk about what you had for lunch before the talk. Just make a connection with the audience.

Move around

Don't just park yourself safely behind a lectern. This may be controversial advice, because a lot of speaking coaches will tell you not to wander all over the stage when giving a talk, but my primary audience is children and they bore easily. For that matter, adults have pretty short attention spans these days, too.

When I'm presenting, I move around, point at the slides, hold up props, walk over to audience members and hand them things to pass around. I've even been known to demonstrate different animal gaits by trotting and galloping across the stage.

Carry Props

It keeps the talk more interesting if you can show people something tangible, not just pictures.

Be flexible

Sometimes, an event is all about the talk. When a store books me into an amphitheater, I know I need to be prepared for a formal talk with a slide presentation. When signing in a store, however, realize that sometimes the talk simply won't happen. If you get a "crowd" of three people, don't just give up and declare there won't be a talk. Instead, walk away from the slides and sit down with your fans. They'll remember that one-on-one (or one-on-several) time with you and it will mean a lot more to them than the slide presentation would have meant anyway.

Engage your audience

Ask them questions. I like to ask where people are from at the beginning and make references to their home states or countries later during the talk. Address people directly. And when you ask them a question, *listen to the answer.* Be the personable, friendly presenter that connects with the audience as people, not the detached robot presenting by rote.

Fans want good books, but they want authors they can connect with, too. You'd be amazed how often I hear things like "Does Craig Johnson have any new books? He's such a nice guy!" It matters.

Craig Johnson: He's a nice guy.

Craig is also big on making himself at home. No matter how big a table we give him, he's going to end up signing books on his lap. He's as likely to sit on the table as he is to sit behind it. This gives his events a very homey and informal feeling that his fans absolutely love.

Tips & Tricks From the Pros

When I'm doing a reading/signing, I always try to be as engaging as possible, especially when it comes to a reading. I try to "perform" rather than read the excerpt. I also keep the excerpt relatively short, about three to five minutes, and use the time to talk about how the book (or selected scene) came to be, and leave plenty of time to converse with the attendees. Those are my favorite kinds of readings/signings to attend as well.

I think we've all had that reading/signing where only one or two people showed up, myself included. I treated those, and the attendee(s) exactly as I would have if 100 people had showed up.

Elisa Lorello, author of *Faking It*, *She Has Your Eyes*, *Ordinary World*, and other works.

Practicing pays off

I am not a "read from my notes" kind of guy. I think it sounds awkward and stilted, and when you are reading from notes you aren't looking at your audience. If I know my subject matter — and I had better — then all I need is an outline to make sure I don't forget anything important.

I always print that outline in big enough print that I can glance surreptitiously at it without having to stop, lift the outline, and squint at it.

That makes it easy to tailor the talk to the audience, since I am speaking extemporaneously anyway. Spending an hour or so customizing the slides makes it look like you have really put forth an effort, and that's the kind of little thing that gets you invited back.

I have two tips, and they're both important. First, I've given readings to three hundred people and readings to three. Give them the same enthusiasm and attention either way. Don't punish the people who did come for the people who didn't, and don't embarrass yourself or the bookseller by being disrespectful or petulant. In this day and age, I like to think that it's always a miracle if anybody shows up at all.

Second, don't read–rather, don't *just* read. They'll get to read the book if they buy it. Your job is to get them to buy it. Make a connection with your audience. Tell them stories that didn't make it into the book, or talk about the genesis of the book or your research or the characters' motivations. Find the human elements and connect with your audience on a human level. Make eye contact. Make time for questions. And make them laugh.

I often go out for drinks after readings, and I like to invite the audience to join me. I always have fun. Some will come and some won't, but I'll bet they'll all remember me when they see my next book for sale somewhere. Anyway, if you don't want to connect with readers, you're writing for all the wrong reasons.

C.B. Bernard, author of *Chasing Alaska: A Portrait of the Last Frontier Then and Now*.

Questions you'll probably be asked

There are questions I've been asked at my talks and signings that you'll probably never hear ("Is that *real* bear poop on your table?"), but there are a lot more questions that just about every author will get at some point. You might want to think about these and have an answer ready for when it comes up.

Note: All of these are actual questions I've been asked at an event. As Dave Barry might say, I'm not making this up.

Did you write this book, or are you just here signing it?

Really? I'm sitting here under a big sign that says "Meet the Author." My picture is on the sign. And I'm autographing books for people. The only thing I can tell you about this is to avoid the snarky response that's inside you, scratching to get out. Unless snarky smart-ass is your persona, in which case go for it!

Do we have to pay for the book?

I forgive the little kids who ask this question. I'm sure they haven't been trained in the ways of capitalism yet. But adults? It's hard to resist the snarky answer: Of course not! I may look like a typical author, but I'm really a wealthy philanthropist and I spend my days writing books and giving them away for free!

Some of the serious and logical questions have quick and easy answers, others more complex:

How long did it take you to write this book?

I adjust my answer to this one based on how they ask it. Some people are asking how long you actually spent hunched over a computer keyboard, typewriter, or stack of parchment pouring out your soul. Others are looking for elapsed time. How long was it from the day you wrote "Chapter 1" at the top of a blank page until the day you held the bound book in your hands?

Sometimes you can give a one-sentence answer to this question, and sometimes it will spawn a seemingly endless stream of follow-up questions where you'll end up describing in excruciating detail the trip that your manuscript made through editor, copy editor, proofreader, fact checker, illustrator, peer reviewer, indexer, cover designer, layout designer, the publisher's cousin's hairdresser, the final galley review, the pressman, that dude in the mail room, and a UPS driver named Lynna who carried the first box of author copies through a snowbank (Lynna rocks!).

Have a few anecdotes ready.

Where do you get your ideas?

How do you answer a question like that? There's no single generic answer, so your best bet is to come up with an anecdote. "That opening scene came from something I actually saw during a ride-along with a local sheriff," or "the monster in the fifth chapter is based on the shadows that the tree outside my childhood bedroom window used to cast on my wall during thunderstorms."

Did you do the drawings?

If you've written an illustrated book, even if the illustrator's name is on the cover as large as your own, someone will ask you if you drew the illustrations.

When I'm asked that question, I tell people that I wish I had the talent that Eli Clark and Rob Rath have. They are the ones that have illustrated my *Who Pooped?* series: Eli did the first six, and Rob has done the others. They are both very skilled, and they are a big part of the reason the books have succeeded.

If you did do the drawings, then be prepared for the immediate follow-up, especially from kids or hard-core fans: "Will you draw me a picture?" If you're the kind of artist that can dash off a sketch quickly, I'd recommend telling them to buy a book and you'll draw a picture in it.

Where's the bathroom?

I don't care if you're sitting directly under a sign that says "Bathrooms are in the back of the store." At some point, someone will walk up to you and ask where the bathrooms are.

Tips & Tricks From the Pros

Tip for making a book signing/reading work well: planning and practice. The best results I've had from readings is when I took the time to carefully plan what I wanted to say and read, and then thoroughly practice, out loud (and in front of a mirror even better) the whole spiel. So that no notes are necessary. When that is done, any ad-libbing I did afterward and in Q&A sessions came easily, confidently, and with apparent authority.

When I was new in my career as a published author, I was scheduled to do a book talk/reading at the Pacific Northwest Booksellers Association—at noon, sandwiched between well-known and popular speakers in a day full of inspirational and educational sessions. With a history of stage fright, feeling very nervous, I hoped for one of two things. A room full of people or no one at all. I didn't get my wish. One person was in attendance. Having been told that the session was being recorded, I decided I must go ahead with it. I have little memory of what I said, but I'm sure it wasn't pretty.

Later on, I had a similar situation at a chain store in Billings, MT. At first I thought no one would show up, but at the last minute, three women came. I went ahead with my planned reading and talk, making it conversational and personal. The women bought books, and one, a teacher at a private school, used them in the classroom and later invited me to come speak to her students.

Janet Muirhead Hill, publisher and author of numerous books, including the *Starlight* series.

How to Sign a Book

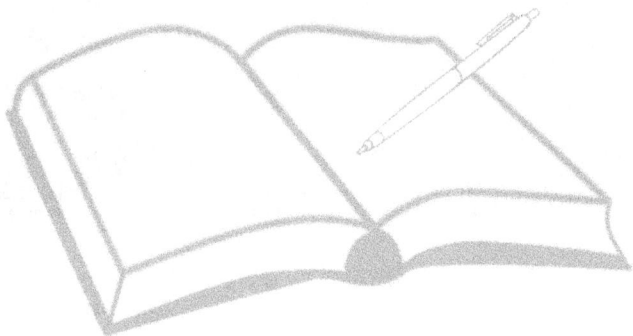

CHAPTER 7

Signing a book seems like a pretty simple concept until the first time somebody hands you a book to sign. Your brain shuts down. You're not sure where to sign or what to write. Does it matter which pen you use? Do you include your middle name? Are you supposed to write something clever? *Oh my God, I forgot my name!*

It pays to think these things through before your first event so that you can be ready.

What page do you sign on?

I think it's best to sign on the title page of the book, somewhere close to where your name appears. If you're signing an anthology that has one of your stories or essays in it, sign on the page where your story starts — again, right by your name. In that case, make sure to memorize what page your story is on, or have someone go through the books beforehand and put a Post-It on that page for you.

IKE
An American Hero
Michael Korda

HARPER
An Imprint of HarperCollins*Publishers*
www.harpercollins.com

In this example, even if you can't read Michael Korda's signature, it's obvious that it matches the name printed right underneath. The signature isn't a gigantic testament to the author's ego, overwhelming everything else on the page (see Orson Scott Card's signature on page 89), nor is it a timid scrawl tucked unnoticed into a corner. It's well-balanced and professional, perfect both for the book and for the author's persona.

Gary D. Robson

Sometimes it can be difficult to sign close to your name. Have no fear, we'll be talking a bit about crowded title pages and title pages with a dark background later in this chapter.

When you have a co-author or illustrator, that adds another reason to put your signature near your name. I have a copy of *The Dog Who Loved Tortillas* signed by the author, Benjamin Alire Sáenz. Should I ever meet the illustrator, Geronimo Garcia, there's plenty of room under his name for him to sign, because Benjamin put his signature above their names.

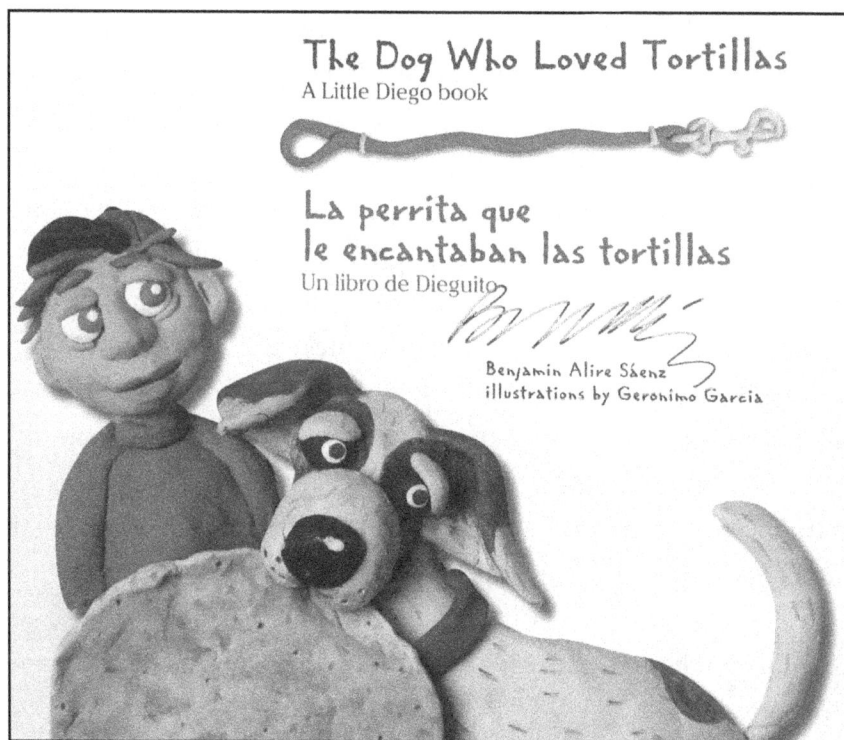

Crossing off your name

I've noticed over the years that some authors will cross off their typeset name when they sign the book. Sometimes, it's a simple line through their name, and sometimes it's a part of the signature, like this:

By Jeffrey Melvin Hutchins

Jeff Hutchins

I've asked quite a few authors why they do it, and most say that they're doing it because that's how they thought it was supposed to be done, or because a favorite author of theirs always crosses out their name when they sign.

As it turns out, there are two other reasons for doing this. One is part of an age-old tradition from the days of calling cards, and it applies to people who go by a nickname or shortening of their name. Crossing off "Jeffrey Melvin Hutchins" and signing "Jeff Hutchins" is a way of saying, "my name is Jeffrey, but you can call me Jeff." It makes the signature more personal and less formal.

Another way of knocking the formality down a notch is to introduce your signature with something like "your friend, Jeff Hutchins."

This "informalization" can be used when signing books to friends, or when inserting a very personal message, as Bill Wyman did here:

For Gary and Kathy who come good enough to make their book seem more important than anything [awards?] after it.

with deep thanks

High Country

A Novel

Bill Wyman

Willard Wyman

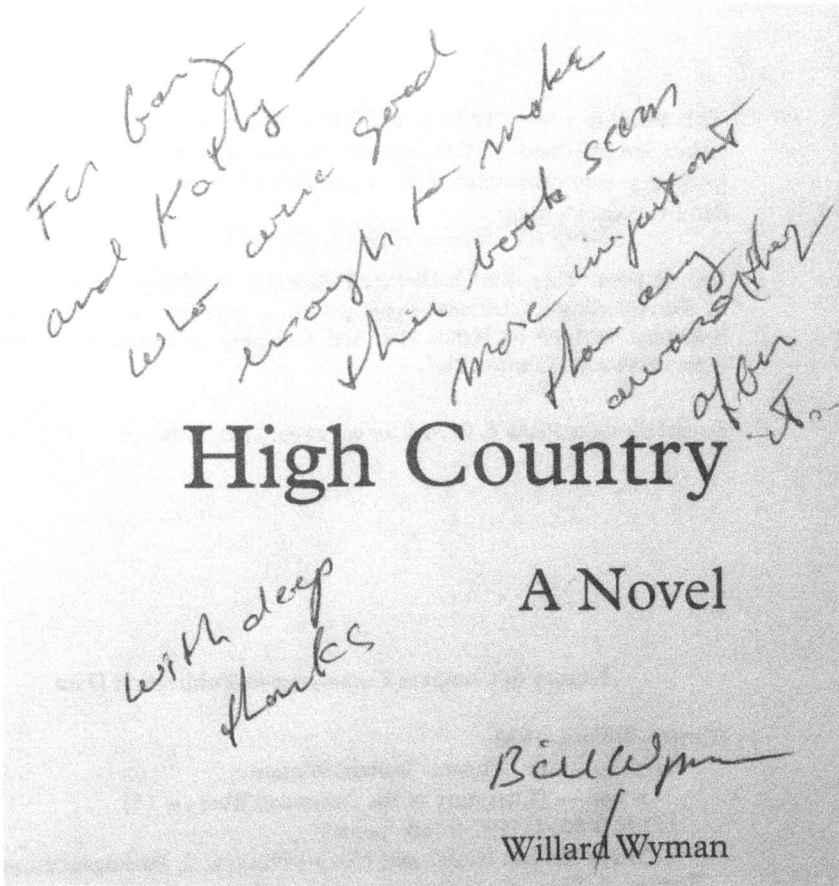

Other authors may place their signature directly on top of their printed name, either for artistic reasons, to link the signature to the name, or as one author told me, to make sure the signature can't be scanned and added to a legal document.

Sometimes, depending upon the book design, you may have trouble finding a place to fit your signature. The title page can be crowded with text and illustrations, or printed on a dark color where your signature won't show up. If that happens, you can either sign on a different page, or come up with a creative solution that incorporates your signature into the design of the page, as Craig Thompson had to do on *Space Dumplins*. See the signature on the planet on page 85?

BONE FIRE

Mark Spragg

There is no one way to sign over your name. Mark Spragg, for example, overlaps his printed name, while Brandon Sanderson totally engulfs it in the signature.

BOOK TWO OF MISTBORN

BRANDON SANDERSON

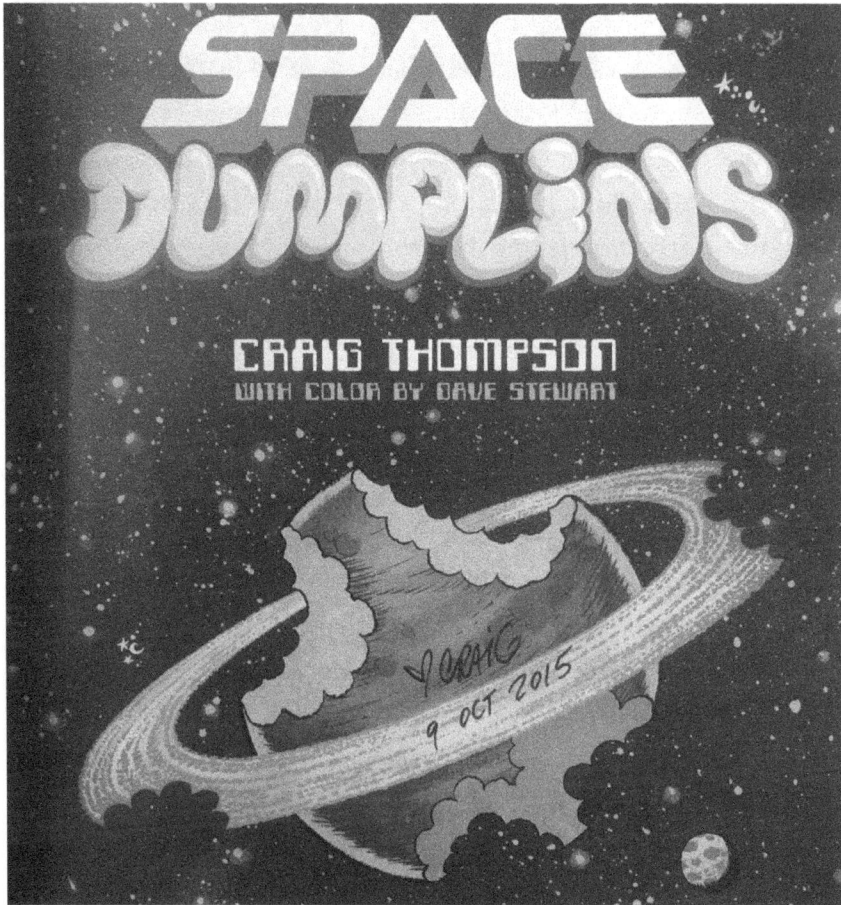

As for the dark background, that leads us right into our next question: what kind of a pen should you use in your signings?

Picking a pen

Selecting a pen is one of the most personal and subjective decisions you'll make for your signings. Some authors will use any pen that happens to be at hand. Others have their "lucky pen" that travels to all signings, or a particular brand or style that they buy by the box so they always have spares.

Susan isn't the only author that loves her Sharpies, but I've seen everything from fine-tip Pilots to expensive Cross pens to

My suggestions are kind of generic: bring a good Sharpie, give everyone a few moments of your time and ask what brought them to the reading, if appropriate, check in advance to make sure the books will be at the store–do so a week before the reading AND two or three days before to make sure they arrived.

***

Susan Kushner Resnick, author of *You Saved Me, Too: What a Holocaust Survivor Taught Me about Living, Dying, Fighting, Loving, and Swearing in Yiddish.*

intricate fountain pens—personally, I carry a pen my son gave me that's carved to look like a black bear when I'm signing my *Who Pooped in the Park?* books.

Here are a few things to take into consideration when selecting your signing pen:

- 📖 Make sure the pen has permanent ink that won't smear or bleed. Otherwise, you'll sign a book and end up with a reverse imprint of it on the facing page, or worse, a big smear where the signature should be.

- 📖 Use a colored pen. Using blue (or the creative color of your choice) makes your signature stand out from the typically monochromatic title page, and also makes it more obvious that the book was hand-signed.

- 📖 If you love a particular pen, as opposed to being happy signing with anything that leaves an ink trail on the paper, then carry one with you all the time. Even if you're not the best-known author in the world, people will recognize you and come up to you asking for signatures when you're not at a formal event. I once had a family rush up to me on a hiking trail in the middle of Yellowstone National Park to have me sign the book they'd just purchased.

Every writer should have that experience of being recognized. It's an amazing feeling. When I was having breakfast with my wife the morning after a signing event, someone who missed the book signing came up with a book she'd purchased in the gift shop and hadn't gotten signed. She recognized me, of course, by my ruggedly handsome face and thoughtful, intelligent demeanor. It had nothing whatsoever to do with the *Who Pooped in the Park?* t-shirt I was wearing.

Yep, that's my story and I'm sticking to it.

Tips & Tricks from the Pros

If your memory is as bad as mine, I would have a sign reading: "If you want me to inscribe the book to you, please tell me your name unless you are a member of my immediate family, and even then it probably wouldn't hurt."

Ed Kemmick, author of *The Big Sky, By and By: True Stories, Real People and Strange Times in the Heart of Montana.*

If your book has a dark-colored background on the title page (I told you we'd get back to this), you can just sign on its verso page, which is the typically blank left-hand page that faces the title page. Or, you can get a bit more creative and use a silver pen, as Toni Yuly did in her book, *Early Bird.*

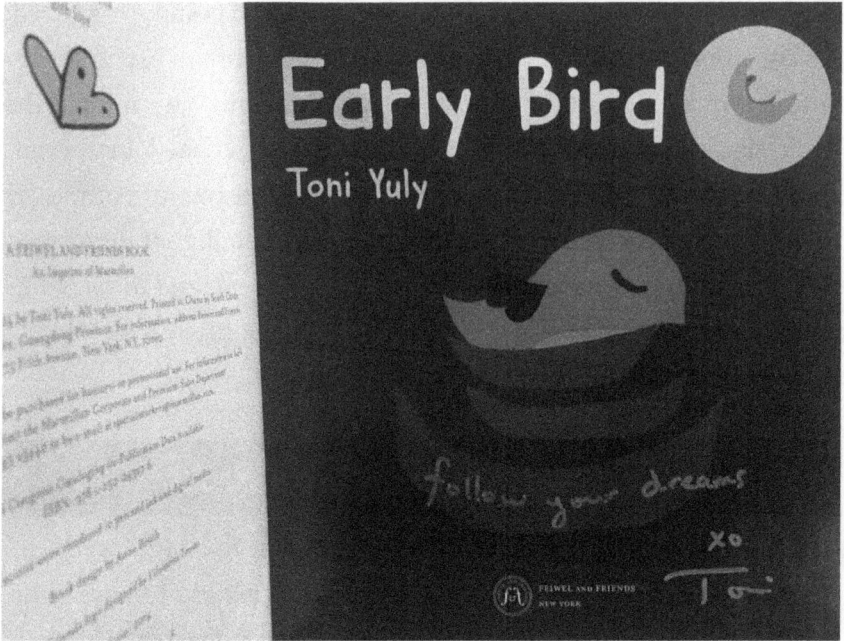

There's something special and magical about a glittery silver signature, but those pens are a bit on the pricey side.

Dating the signature

Generally, I don't write the date when I sign a book unless I know it's for a special occasion ("would you sign this to Anne for her birthday?") or I'm specifically asked to date it.

One exception is when the book is brand new, especially for novels. There's something special about owning a first edition that was signed and dated by the author the month it came out, and collectors prize books signed on the release date. Be prepared for people to want their picture taken with you at the release party as evidence that their book really is a first edition, first printing.

Some authors even number their signatures for the first 100 copies or so that they sign of each book. It doesn't take much extra effort, and some people will be very excited to have the first (or even the fifty-first) autographed copy of your book.

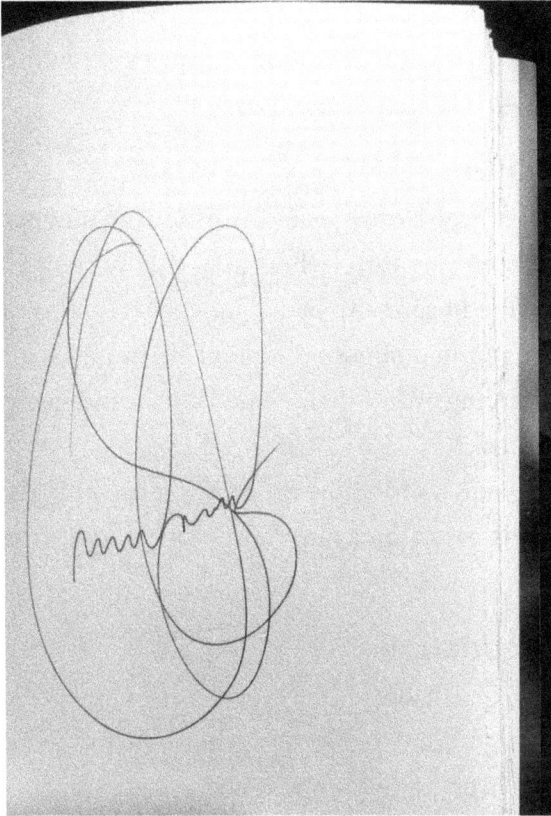

This is Orson Scott Card's signature in my copy of "A War of Gifts." He couldn't put it on the title page because the signature requires an entire page of its own.

Legibility

Slow down. I believe that a customer who traveled to my book event deserves more than an illegible scrawl. I try to make whatever I write readable.

There's a side benefit to slowing down a bit. When you write fast, you make mistakes. If you goof up the inscription, you have just ruined the book, and that's going to cost you.

At my last book signing in the lobby of the Old Faithful Inn in Yellowstone Park, I was writing quickly to work my way through a crowd. I was also talking at the same time as I wrote, which is a surefire way to get distracted and goof up. Sure enough, that's what I did. Even though bookstores buy my books at a 40% discount, the gift shop there in the Inn charged me full price for the book I'd ruined. Depending on your royalty rate, one full price screw-up will cost you your royalties from ten or more books.

Your "official" signature

At a writer's conference, I once asked a group of authors whether they used the same signature when they sign a book as they do when they sign a credit card slip or a legal document. I was greeted by a moment of stunned silence. None of them had ever thought about someone buying one of their signed books and using the signature to forge a check.

I don't know if this matters to you—especially since nobody even looks at credit card signatures anymore—but I use two different signatures.

Don't just sign; personalize

If someone is going out of their way to come to your book signing event, don't just sign your name. Ask who they'd like the book signed to, and add a little note of some kind.

With my *Who Pooped in the Park?* books, I usually write "Watch where you step" unless people ask me to do something else. That makes my life easier, as I'm not scrambling to think of something clever for each book I sign, and people really seem to like it.

I have absolutely no idea what I'm going to write when I sign this book. How do you sign a book about signing books? I'm tempted to do it all wrong, just for the irony (I know, that's not really irony, but let's not get into that here). Be prepared to have this book signed upside-down on the Table of Contents page with your name misspelled.

You have to be careful when your book covers a somber subject, as in Michael Punke's *Fire and Brimstone* and my own *The Darkest Hour*. A quote from the book or a popular phrase that doesn't appear to make light of a disaster is the best way to go.

FIRE AND BRIMSTONE

Tap 'er light —

The

North Butte

Mining Disaster

of 1917

Michael Punke

MICHAEL PUNKE

08/10/06

This is a good time to reinforce something I said earlier in this chapter: slow down and pay attention! I was chatting with some people who had just bought a copy of *Who Pooped in the Northwoods?*, and they grabbed a copy of *The Darkest Hour* and asked me to sign that, too. Being completely distracted, I wrote "Watch where you step" in *The Darkest Hour* — not the somber sentiment I had intended.

Now I stop and think before setting pen to title page. If I'm signing *Myths & Legends of Tea*, I write "enjoy these stories with a good cup of tea." If I'm signing *The Darkest Hour*, I write "never again." I may improvise when I'm personalizing, but having these phrases in my mind may help keep me from ruining a book.

Be prepared with several little tag lines, and also be ready to explain this process to people that don't understand it. More than once, I've had somebody ask me to write something like, "Happy birthday from Grandma and Grandpa," and I have to explain that I'm signing it from me, not from them. They are welcome to add their own inscription as well, but the point of a book signing is to get the author's signature, not the gift-giver's.

JAILBAIT

ZOMBIE

Better undead than unread,

Mario Acevedo

Mario's take on the smiley face is perfect for his book!

Mario Acevedo, author of *Jailbait Zombie*, not only came up with a clever tag line to go with his signature, but included a simple drawing as well, to make it even more personal.

Allie Brosh, author of *Hyperbole and a Half*, did a book signing at a book conference cocktail party I attended. I'm not sure if it was just the setting (or the wine), or if she's always like that, but she went above and beyond the call of duty — way above — by offering to draw a picture of an animal on the title page of her book for anyone who asked. Any animal you asked for! I requested a jackalope, the legendary denizen of the West with the body of a jackrabbit and the antlers of a deer.

I like to think I was the first person to ask
Allie Brosh to draw a jackalope.

Sometimes, though, raising the bar can come back to bite you in the butt.

At a Cheetah Conservation Fund event years ago, I met Tippi Hedren, the actress who became famous for the Alfred Hitchcock film, The Birds. She had written a book called *The Cats of Shambala*, and I bought a copy. When she signed it for me, she added three simple little birds around her signature (see the picture under the book cover below). I told her the birds were really a cute touch.

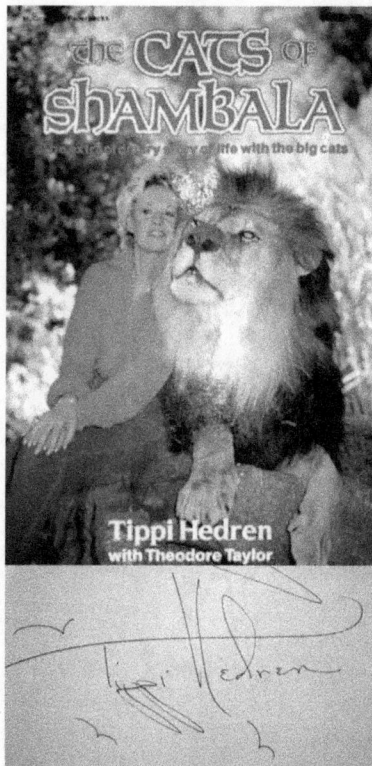

The cover to Tippi Hedren's book
and her signature with the birds.

"I wish I'd never started that," she said.

When I asked why, she told me about when she first started drawing little birds. It was a random thing. Sometimes she'd draw

Gary D. Robson

two, sometimes three, sometimes four. Then, when she drew two birds by her signature in a book one day, a fan complained.

"How come my friend got three birds in her book and I only got two in mine?"

The little birds had stopped being a cute improvisation and became a part of her signature; an expectation rather than an extra.

It's a good thing she hadn't drawn a pride of lions!

Tips & Tricks from the Pros

1. Always sign the Title page or the Series Title Page…it just makes sense.

2. Add specifics of where and when you are signing e.g. "London Academy, January 2016," it adds to the atmosphere of the recollection when the page is reopened.

3. Don't be shy; a signed book is a special thing and your signature enhances its personal value to the recipient, so fill the page if you need.

4. Take your time, appreciate the recipient's enthusiasm, take time to have a moment of connection with them out of respect.

5. Double-triple check the spelling of the name I once signed three books before getting Kathie right. I ended up waiting for a Cathy and Kathy to come along…

Kevin Gascoyne, author of *Tea: History, Terroirs, Varieties* and other tea books.

The Book Signing

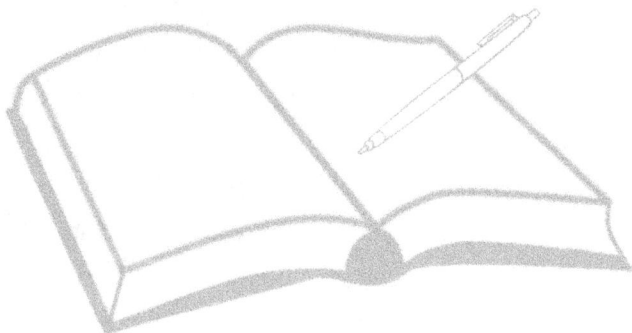

CHAPTER 8

You've made it. You've arrived at the event venue, given your talk (if you're doing one), and settled at your signing table. The first interested reader walks up to the table, looks you in the eye, and says, "I'll take one of those books!" Now what do you do?

Hopefully, you've already turned off or silenced your phone and eliminated any other distractions that might prevent you from giving 100% of your attention to the people in front of you. They've gone to the trouble of attending your event; you need to put in the effort to make them feel like it was worth it.

Why you're really there

If you do the math, the royalties you make on copies sold at the book signing are rarely enough to cover your expenses in getting to the event. You aren't there to make a pile of cash in royalties at the signing; you are there for public relations.

Treating the customers well is such an obvious rule that I almost hesitate to include it. People will tell their friends about the fascinating, polite, pleasant author that talked with them and signed their book. They will tell a lot more friends if you were rude or indifferent.

I once invited a well-known New York City author to do a signing at my store. He laughed in my face and said, "Me? Go to a store in Montana?" It wasn't a chuckle, a chortle, or a guffaw; it was a full-fledged belly laugh that went on long enough to make me thoroughly uncomfortable.

He did this in front of a dozen other booksellers at a conference luncheon (they were pretty uncomfortable with the situation, too). If he had politely accepted my business card and said he'd see what he could do, I wouldn't have thought any less of him. A lot of authors don't want to make the trip to a small town far from home. As it is, I've told that story to dozens of people, and the booksellers that were seated at the table with us—most of them also residents of "fly-over states"—probably have as well. It wouldn't have taken him any effort to be pleasant instead of coming across as an arrogant buffoon.

But there's another purpose for your book signing tour that's just as important in the long run: developing relationships with the bookstore staff. Treat them well and earn their respect, and the long-term payoff is far greater than what you get the day of the event.

Your publisher can help you with that relationship building. After all, increasing sales of your books is their goal as well.

I did a book signing at the Grand Canyon Visitor Center on the South Rim in 2006. We didn't have much swag at the time, so the only thing I brought along for my table was a sign. I arrived at the event to find all of the store staff wearing Who Pooped in the Park? t-shirts. I didn't even know we had t-shirts.

As it turned out, Farcountry Press had decided to try making some shirts, and they surprised me by sending them to the store without telling me. The staff was in on the surprise, and thoroughly enjoyed my stupefied look when I saw them.

I don't think I've ever felt quite so much like a rock star as I did when they all asked me to sign their shirts — just look at my face in the picture (I'm the one without a *Who Pooped* t-shirt on).

How to make a signing work

Talk to people

It never ceases to amaze me when authors come in, plant themselves behind the signing table, and curl up as inconspicuously as possible. You are there to promote your book. So *promote!* Chat with people. Introduce yourself. Tell them you are in the store signing books. Recommend a book (even if it's not yours). Ask their names.

You will be rejected sometimes, of course. There will always be people walking by with their heads carefully averted to avoid making eye contact. There will be people who glance at your book, say something dismissive, and move on. But there will be far more people that will exchange a few pleasant words with you, remember you in the future, and possibly buy one of your books.

Don't be pushy, though. If someone does start to walk away, don't try to stop them. You're being pleasant and friendly, not being a loud street vendor hawking goods to passersby.

While you're at it, engage the staff. Be pleasant. Chat with them (when there isn't a customer waiting). Offer to sign a book for them. Make them want to send customers over to your table. This will pay off in spades the next day when they're telling everyone how wonderful you were and showing off your books. The signing is only the beginning. If they like you (and you wrote a decent book, of course), then they'll still be hand-selling your books long after you leave the store.

On the flip side, don't monopolize the staff. Keeping the employees from doing their job does not lead to happy store managers!

Hand customers your book

People are much more likely to buy something once they've handled it. Say something about the book, and then put it in the customer's hands. Let them look through it while you talk about it.

When customers are nearby, stay near the table

When hosting signings in my store, I've gotten customers interested in a book, and then not been able to find the author to sign a copy. Don't wander away unless you tell the bookstore staff where you're going and when you'll be back.

Don't undercut or bypass the store

Want to piss off a store owner? Hand out bookmarks that say "available at Amazon." Tell people they can get your other books at the store down the street. Tell customers to call you direct for more copies instead of coming back to the store. Even worse, sell books out of your trunk right after the signing. The store has worked hard to put this event together, spent money on promotion, and showed their faith in you by providing space in the store. Return the favor and send them business.

A few specific notes for children's authors

There are a lot of things that are different for an author who writes books for children—especially picture books.

No cursive. I was born in 1958, so handwriting was a big thing in school. We learned to write beautiful cursive script, and that's what our generation uses for formal occasions. Today's children, however, are often not taught cursive. Schools in our area have dropped it, and many others around the country as well. If you handwrite a clever little note to the children, odds are they won't be able to read it. This doesn't apply to the signature itself, but...

Sign on the title page near where your name appears. When the child is looking at the book, they see your name printed in the book and your name signed close by. The younger the child, the harder time they have grasping that you're the person who created this book. That proximity of printed name and signature helps reinforce it.

This is how I usually sign "Who Pooped" books.

If you're the illustrator, draw something. It doesn't need to be anything fancy. Even a little smiley face like Mario Acevedo uses (see page 92). *What* you drew doesn't matter. What matters is that you drew it *just for them*.

Use a clearer signature. When I'm signing a check or a legal document, my signature is a scrawl. If you didn't already know my name, you'd never be able to decipher the signature. As grown-ups, we get this. An illegible scribble is the standard for signatures. Little kids don't necessarily get it. If the family is plopping down $11.95 for a copy of my book, I figure the least I can do is make it readable. I know kids who don't read cursive won't be able to read a signature, but the letters are close enough to identify if you know what you're looking for. Speaking of which...

Always include the child's name. You probably do this anyway, but it's doubly important for little children. One of the first things they will learn to spell and recognize is their own name, and it's infinitely cool to them when they see their own name in the book.

Always ask them to spell their names. Again, you probably already do this, but it's more important with children's books. If you are signing a book for a 60-year-old named Ellen, it's almost a sure bet that her name is spelled E-L-L-E-N. Young parents today are much more likely to use unique (strange, odd, phonetic...) spellings than their parents or grandparents. A six-year-old with that name is much more likely than previous generations to spell it Ellyn or Elin or Ellan or Ellin or Elhen or Elen.

Talk directly to the child. I see far too many authors of children's books that speak to the parents and barely make eye contact with the kids. The book is for the kids. The experience is for the kids. Ask children what their names are and how to spell them, and look to the parents for confirmation if you can't understand. Children are used to being ignored by grown-ups. Be the exception.

Helpers

At a really busy book signing with a popular author, having an assistant at the table can make a huge difference for everyone. Make sure the author isn't seated too close to the cash register, so there's plenty of room for two separate lines. Then set up two chairs at the table and arrange it so that the people in line reach the assistant first.

Getting spellings of names for the author

I've already mentioned the importance of spelling people's names right. The assistant can talk to each customer and make sure the names for the inscription are written neatly on a piece of paper for the author, along with any special requests.

Opening to the correct page

If the book is a hardback, someone should "flap" the books in advance, finding the page where the author prefers to sign and putting the front flap of the book jacket there. When the author is ready to sign, it's easy to open the book to the correct page.

With paperbacks, you can accomplish the same thing using a promotional bookmark or using that piece of paper with the names on it—assuming they were written with quick-drying ink on paper that won't smudge!

Tips for a successful book signing: Dress up a little. Remember, people take the time to shave and comb their hair before they come to see you. You can do more. As the Sisters in Crime handbook on book signings (*Shameless Promotion for Brazen Hussies*) points out: You're the star. Shine a little.

Margaret Coel, author of the Wind River mystery series.

ATTITUDE

Careful what you say and who you say it in front of!

Some book signings do well and some don't, no matter how well you prepare. And some stores are larger than others as well.

An author came into my store for a book signing. From the beginning, it was clear that she was used to dealing with much larger stores. She hadn't told me in advance that she needed a projector screen, and didn't arrive early enough to give me time to fetch one.

I decided that the best move would be to take down the big sign behind my tea bar and let her aim the projector at the blank wall behind it. I went into the back room to get my ladder, and she pulled out her cell phone and made a call. Doug, the tea bar manager, had coincidentally gone back in the kitchen for a moment.

We got the projector hooked up and adjusted. A bit later, when the author went out to her car for a moment, some customers that were seated in the tea bar pulled Doug aside.

"Do you know what that author said when you were both out of the room?"

"No," Doug responded.

"She made some comment about being in the middle of nowhere and asked her husband why they even bothered to come to this place."

I suppose it never occurred to her that in a small town indie bookstore, the customers sitting at the table might be friends of the owners.

Needless to say, this exchange made us feel rather uncomfortable when she came back in the store. Because I like her book and was looking forward to the talk, I didn't say anything to her.

As it turned out, this was one of those rare events where nobody shows up. Where most authors would be setting up a table

Tales from the Front Lines

I had one author, published through a major publisher, who came to do a book signing during the bookstore's biggest night of the year: our University Staff and Faculty night. We'd get 2-3,000 people who come those evenings. We book three authors to do a signing those nights.

He came in, sat down and started pulling attitude with me from the beginning because he had to share the spotlight with two other authors. He complained that not enough people were coming to talk to him about his book (see above). He was nearly contemptuous of the other authors, me, and the customers. His attitude with the customers was awful and he wouldn't personalize books, and he finally got up and left a half hour early, because he said, "this was a waste of my time."

Drew Goodman, former bookstore manager at University of Utah bookstore and Borders.

and engaging everyone who came in the store, she hung back and stood by the projector. When customers came in, I told them about the book and encouraged them to take a look. I had to specifically ask her to come over and engage.

After 15 minutes, there was nobody sitting down waiting for her talk. She declared that since nobody was there for her presentation, she was leaving. I talked her into staying another 20 minutes or so, and then she signed a pre-sold book and left, even though the event was scheduled to go on for another hour.

As an author, I've done book signings where we didn't sell anything, but I never packed up and left early. I never stopped trying to engage a customer. And I definitely never bad-mouthed the store or the town.

As a bookseller, I've had big-name authors in my store who didn't get enough people to justify standing up and giving a talk. What did they do? Sit down and engage with people one-on-one. Offer to sign stock. Talk to the employees about their books. Do pretty much anything but trash-talk the store and leave early.

Either this author didn't realize that my customers might actually talk to me, or she didn't care. When her publisher called the next day to see how the signing went, I passed on that little story.

Tales from the Front Lines

On my way to Vroman's bookstore in Pasadena, I was shocked to find a line of people a block long outside the store! Good heavens. For me? No, sadly. Bill Clinton had done an earlier signing and he was still signing for the crowds.

Margaret Coel, author of the Wind River mystery series.

But what if nobody shows up?

I wish I could predict how many people will be at a signing or talk, but I can't. I've had some amazing authors in the store that only drew one or two people, and some unknown self-published authors that drew big crowds. Sometimes, the weather affects attendance. Sometimes, the promotion just didn't get that viral "click" where everyone is telling everyone else about it. Sometimes, another business sets up an event at the same time.

Low sales don't mean your book sucks. It doesn't mean there's anything wrong with you. And it doesn't necessarily mean the store didn't promote the event. Sometimes, you just don't catch a break.

Tales from the Front Lines

When Linc [co-author Lincoln Child] and I were touring for our first novel, *Relic*, we were split up and toured individually. In one book signing in Minnesota, Linc's mother was the only one who showed up; and that same week, at a signing Linc did in Cambridge, Mass, my mother was the only one to show up.

Douglas Preston, author of dozens of books, including the bestselling *Pendergast* series with Lincoln Child.

After the Signing

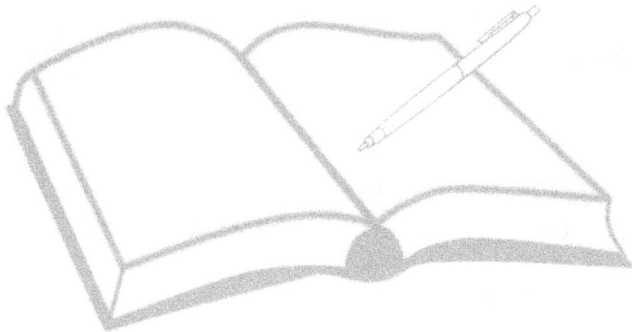

The signing has wrapped up. Your time is over. The staff is cleaning up. What do you do next? Well, first, don't let the staff clean up by themselves. Help out. Carry books. Throw away any detritus from the signing. Show them that you're there to work, too.

Never complain about sales at the signing

There are a million reasons that a book event can go south. It happens to absolutely everyone, even the big names.

No matter what happened or whose fault it was, griping about poor sales won't make it better. Be gracious about it, accept part of the blame even if it's not your fault (no, especially if it's not your fault), and move on.

I know. Sometimes it's quite difficult to stay calm and deal with it. Sometimes, it's just an unmitigated disaster and you really want to yell at someone.

CHAPTER 9

Tales from the Front Lines

My worst bookstore signing was probably at the Borders where the woman in charge hadn't even ordered my books. I drove 200 miles out of my way to do the signing, and she gave some lame excuse like "I just got so busy the last couple of weeks."

Sneed B. Collard III, author of over 75 books, mostly for children and young adults.

That's where it's most important to be gracious. Be remembered as the classy author, not the whiny one.

Offer to sign inventory

Typically, my store will sell as many of your books in the week or two after the signing as we do at the event. You can help to make that happen by staying after the event is done and signing our back stock. It's also a nice touch to keep a package or two of bookplates with you. Then if the store sold out (yippee!) you can sign a few bookplates and leave them.

I've learned another lesson the hard way: promoting an event hard in advance requires you to have more books than you'll sell at the event. We have a saying in the book business: "Stack 'em high and watch 'em fly." It refers to a customer's reluctance to pick up the last book on a table, and to the feeling that if there's a big stack of books, they must be something special.

Last summer, I set up a table right by the front door of my bookstore and posted the book signing schedule for the next month on it. I had stacks of all of the books for the signings arranged on the table. There were a couple of instances where I ordered a dozen copies of the book, thinking that would be plenty for the signing, and sold all of them before the signing even happened. In some instances, I had time to order more. In a couple of other cases, I had to make that horribly embarrassing phone call to the author saying, "do you have more books you can bring?"

A good in-store display will kick off sales in advance of the event itself, both to people who won't be able to make the event and to people who think the book looks interesting but really don't care about author autographs.

Advance sales will pick up even more if the store offers to hold the book with instructions on how to sign it. We hold the personalized books for local customers (always prepaid, as the book can't be sold to someone else once it's personalized), and also offer to ship books to the customer after the signing.

If a store is going to offer this service, someone needs to be on top of making it happen. We've found ourselves several times on the day after a signing realizing that we had a prepaid book that we forgot to have the author sign!

It is also very common for people to come in the day after the signing, saying that they couldn't make it or forgot when it was. We've had customers come in a week after the event because they put the event on their calendar for the wrong Saturday! If there is a stack of signed books in the store, many of these people will buy a copy even though it isn't personalized.

Tales from the Front Lines

Probably my best bookstore signing was when I was doing the *B is for Big Sky Country* book before Christmas at Fact and Fiction bookstore here in Missoula. I signed 20-30 books that night, but she'd sold about 600 copies of it in and around that date.

Sneed B. Collard III, author of over 75 books, mostly for children and young adults.

Signed copies for the staff

Sometimes, people who work in the bookstore might feel that it's unprofessional or inappropriate to approach you to get a book signed. Sometimes, management tells them to wait until the very end to make sure all of the customers get copies. Either way, when you start packing up your signing table, ask the staff if they'd like you to sign books for them. If they say yes, then give them a signature that shows how much you appreciate their help.

Craig Lancaster personalized a copy of *600 Hours of Edward* the first time he came to my store.

What he wrote isn't the reason I've invited him back for every book he's written since, and he was the first author to show up for Indies First at my store as well, but writing "it was a treat to spend an afternoon in your lovely store" made the book into much more than just an autographed copy. It doubled as a thank you note!

Brent Ghelfi is another example of an author that knows how to develop a relationship. His first novel, *Volk's Game*, was on the *New York Times* best seller list when he came to my store in 2007. That doesn't happen often in our tiny little town, so we made a very big deal of the event.

Unfortunately, our advertising and promotion didn't translate into sales. It was a very quiet event, and we sold only a handful of books. During the dead times when there were no customers in the store, he chatted with me and wandered the store.

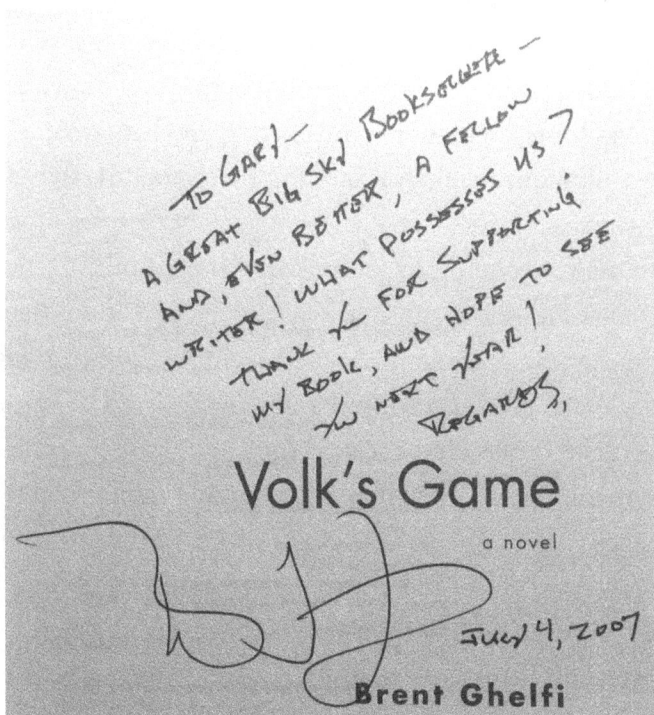

When we wrapped up, instead of complaining about the small turnout and insignificant sales, he thanked me profusely for having him, offered to come back, and wrote an absolutely fantastic inscription in my copy of his book. As I write this, his visit was eight years ago and I'm still recommending his book to people (it helps that it's a good book).

Dance with the one that brung ya

Back in 2006, my bookstore set up a signing with an author whose book fit very well with our store and our area. It was a holiday weekend, with high traffic in the store, and we promoted the event well. We didn't pay her way to Montana, but we did spend money advertising the signing on the radio and in the newspaper. We put up posters around town, set up a display, sent out email alerts, and generally did our best to make sure the book would sell.

Generally speaking, book signings are a medium- to long-term investment for our store. In a very few cases, we'll sell massive stacks of books and show a nice profit. In most cases, we sell some books, raise some awareness, and start a process of selling books over the following weeks or months (or sometimes years). This event was no exception.

The author rolled into town early (a good thing), checked in with us, and said she wanted to wander around town for a while before the signing. The signing itself went well. She engaged the customers, sold books, and generally made a good impression. Then she turned on the hard sell, trying to get us to buy cases of the books from her before she left town. Knowing my market, I bought a small stack... .

She wandered off, and we set up the signing table as a display to further promote her books. Then the red flags began...

I got a call from a store down the street asking how well the signing went. The author was in her store trying to sell her books. A friend with a real estate office popped in to tell me that the author had offered to sell him a case of her books at a 50% discount to give away to clients (she had only offered me 40%). By the end of the day, four local business owners had contacted me to say that she was trying to sell them books, often at lower prices than I had paid.

My wife and I were pissed off. We had invested money promoting the book and the event, and the author was cutting off our follow-up sales, which is where we stood the best chance of recouping our investment.

I'm not saying authors should limit themselves to one store per town. In bigger cities, that would be impossible. But, as we say here in Montana, "Dance with the one that brung ya." If a store is spending money to promote your event, never sell directly to their customers and never undercut their prices. And don't create competition for them that didn't exist before your visit. Red Lodge only has 2,300 people. If someone wants your book, I think they'll find their way to my store.

We boxed up all of her books, put a stop-payment on our check, and mailed the whole kit and caboodle back to her. Since that day, I've told this tale to many booksellers, and encouraged them not to host that author for an event unless she pays all promotional costs. Her book is a nice fit in my store, but there are several others that cover the same subject matter. Had she showed us some modicum of respect, we would probably have sold a lot of her books since her signing. As it was, we'll never sell another copy. Her attempt to undermine us has most likely cost her a lot more than it gained in sales.

I consider her behavior unethical. I've talked to others who disagree with that assessment. Everyone I've discussed this with, however, agrees that it was disrespectful and rude.

Tips for Bookstores

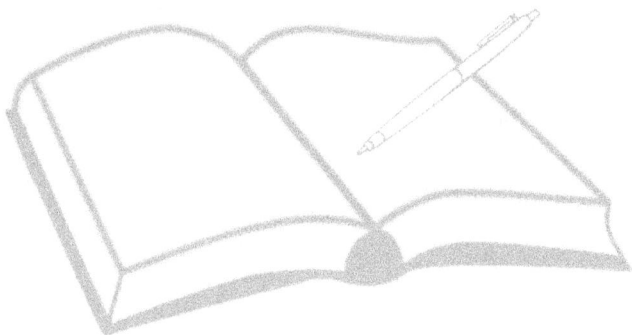

CHAPTER 10

Most of the tips and tricks in this book are aimed at authors. As a bookstore owner, I've made a lot of mistakes, and I've actually learned from some of them! I've also found a lot of things that work well for me.

If you're an author, don't skip this chapter. It's good to understand what goes on across the table from you.

Promote the Event

Policies on paid advertising vary from store to store. Many stores don't have the budget to take out an ad for every author, but there are a lot of forms of free publicity: posters, email newsletters, Facebook, Twitter, displays and signs in the store, and telling customers about it at the register. The more publicity you do, the more books you'll sell.

I had a huge "Book Signing Today" sign made, which I put up in the front window the day of an event. Most events in my store take place in the late afternoon, so that gives a full day of publicity to the signing. I also make smaller 8½ x 11 signs on my ink-jet printer for the event and tape one of those right above the big sign in the window.

There's a table right inside the front door in my store. During the summer, I keep a large calendar of upcoming events posted above the table, with stacks of books for the next half-dozen signings. It's common to sell as many books from that table as I do at the signing itself.

Get the details right!

I've shown up a stores where a sign had my name spelled wrong. It's right there on the front cover of the book—and it's not a complicated name, either. There's no excuse for goofing up a detail like that. Use the author's name exactly as it appears on the book, including middle initial, honorifics like Dr. or Rev., and nicknames.

If the author does have an unusual name, this can be a major problem. When she signed in my store, Carrie La Seur made a point of thanking me for spelling her name right on the posters and Facebook posts. She shouldn't have to do that. Whether you know how to spell a name or not, you can certainly look at a book cover, or just use copy and paste to pull it from a book database!

Order enough stock

Even returnable books cost money to return. I understand that. In my own store, I won't order a hundred books unless the author is huge. But I will do my best to have enough for a decent display, and enough to satisfy demand. Booksellers need to work with authors. If the store can't justify spending what it costs for a good stock of books, then authors should get a heads-up so they can bring books themselves.

Know where the stock is

Yep. I showed up at a store for a book signing where they had 100 copies of my book on hand, but they couldn't find them.

They weren't out on display; someone had prepared them for the signing, put the boxes of books in the back room, and then gone home without telling the manager where they were. I spent ten awkward minutes chatting with customers while the store staff frantically searched the building for my books.

Prepare the signing area in advance

It's frustrating for an author to show up, ready to start—hopefully with customers gathered in anticipation—only to have no place to sign. Again, this tip is from my own experience. More than once I've hung out in a store talking with customers while waiting for the staff to find a table or chair for me. Ideally, that signing table should be set up well in advance of the signing, with "AUTHOR EVENT" signs and a big stack of books.

Tell your staff what's going on

I was doing a book signing at a big store (not a bookstore, incidentally). When I arrived, there was no sign and none of the clerks working in front knew there was an event that day. The manager was on break, and I stood in front wondering if I was in the wrong store until they tracked him down. Not a great first impression of the store!

Send customers to the table

Whenever you're talking to a customer, say "we have an author in the store doing a book signing." The author can't be expected to run around the whole store flagging down customers. You need to help.

Let the author describe the book

If a customer asks during a signing what the book is all about, let the author answer if she's not busy. Authors can describe their books much better—and are more likely to sell a copy—than you.

Negotiate book discounts and terms in advance

Don't let the situation arise where you get to end of the event, and have the author hand you an invoice at 20% discount payable immediately when you were expecting a 40% discount and net 30 terms. Before authors pull out one book of their own, you should know what it will cost you.

Take special orders in advance

Customers who can't attend the event would love to be able to get a personalized book anyway. Take orders up front, and have the author sign them before or after the event—not while customers are waiting.

You have to be careful to remember those books at the event. I've screwed up (twice!) and found prepaid books on the shelf waiting to be signed after the author had already left.

The number one requirement for a successful book signing is communication. We're all guilty of miscommunication from time to time. I know I screwed up communications with a bookstore once when I had to reschedule a signing. They had a couple of unhappy customers because of it (apparently they had pre-sold some books and had to refund them) and it was my fault.

I've seen bookstores mess up signings, too. In almost every case, good communication up-front would have prevented the problem. Some stores go so far as to draft a policy on signings and send a copy to every author before the event.

Book signings are a partnership. Authors and booksellers need to work together to create successful events.

Gary D. Robson

Multi-Author Events

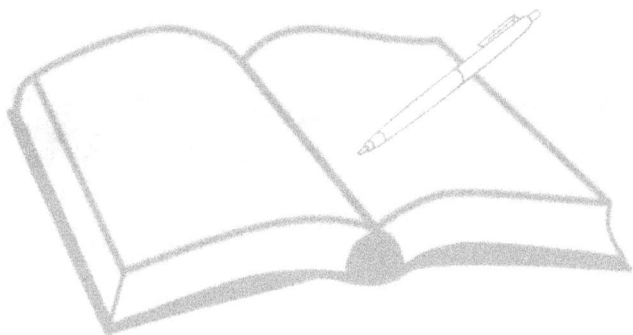

If one is good, two are better, right? Sometimes that can be the case. Especially in a smaller store, it can be difficult to draw a crowd for a relatively unknown author. It's more difficult to coordinate multiple authors for a single event, but it can pay off well in attendance — and sales.

While stores may only get a handful of people at a signing for a new fantasy novel, they could end up with a big crowd for a "fantasy day" event. The store could invite several authors, set up fantasy-themed displays around the store, and possibly offer special deals that day.

Authors can help this process along by banding together and approaching the store together. The common theme doesn't have to be a genre. It's not just "mystery day" or "cookbook day" that can draw attention. It might be a group of authors that all write strong female characters, or feature World War II themes, or all involve train travel. What matters is having an overlapping fan base. I'll have more to say about that later in the chapter.

I was invited to a big event in Grand Teton National Park specifically for authors that wrote books set in and around the Park. There were over twenty of us, and it was a blast. The crowd was far bigger than any one of us could have hoped to draw, and we enjoyed meeting each other and talking as much as we enjoyed selling our books.

Tips & Tricks From the Pros

Probably the best book events I've been involved in have featured more than one author with something in common, and a moderator. Many writers are writers because they'd rather write than talk to people, so expecting them to come up with a great stand-up routine is asking a lot.

Carrie La Seur, author of *The Home Place*.

Signing with your co-authors

If you have a co-author or illustrator, work out in advance where on the page each of you will sign (you should always both sign on the same page). That way, it doesn't matter which author signs first, or even if you sign on different days. When we had Greg Mortenson in our store in 2007 for a Three Cups of Tea event, his co-author, David Relin, wasn't able to attend.

The newly-released paperback copies that we ordered from the publisher, of course, came with no signatures on them. Greg, however, brought along some hardback copies that already had David's signature, and added his own for each customer.

THREE CUPS OF TEA

ONE MAN'S MISSION
TO FIGHT TERRORISM AND BUILD NATIONS...
ONE SCHOOL AT A TIME

For Gary + Kathy –

GREG MORTENSON

and

DAVID OLIVER RELIN

*"The real enemy
is ignorance."*

Signing with authors of other books

Book signings with more than one author can take a lot of forms. Perhaps one of the best ways to get a feeling for this is to contact your favorite indie bookstore and volunteer to participate in their Indies First event the day after Black Friday.

What is Indies First? It started in 2013, when Sherman Alexie (author of *The Absolutely True Diary of a Part-Time Indian*, among other books) wrote an open letter to other authors suggesting that Small

Business Saturday (the day after Black Friday) would be a perfect opportunity for authors to show their support of independent bookstores by becoming an honorary bookseller for a day. He said we could call it "Indies First." His idea went viral. Authors jumped on the idea, and the American Booksellers Association stepped in to help pair up authors with stores.

On Small Business Saturday, which fell on November 30th that year, over 1,000 authors showed up at their favorite bookstore to sell books. Not just their own books, either. These authors did what the people in the stores do every day: they talked to shoppers and helped them pick books for themselves and for gifts.

Craig Lancaster came to my store that day—and it warmed my heart that an author published by Amazon still loves the brick & mortar stores! Craig introduced himself to everyone that came in the store and told them about Indies First. Normally, when Craig is in my store, I'm telling everybody about his books: *Edward Adrift* is as good as (dare I say "better than"?) its predecessor, *600 Hours of Edward*. I really enjoyed his short story collection, *Quantum Physics and the Art of Departure*, as well. That day, however, I got to listen to Craig helping people find good books by other authors. Sure, we sold some of his, but I enjoyed hearing what other authors he recommended.

I think that the Indies First program is a wonderful idea. It does sadden me a bit that we need to do it. A section on a website entitled, "People who looked at this book also bought these books," isn't a substitute for talking to someone who's knowledgeable about books, and that's what indie stores are all about.

Back before I bought a bookstore, I used to seek out the indies because shopping at the big stores was frustrating. I could never find anyone at a chain store who actually knew their inventory or knew how to answer my questions. Even though I own a store now, I still visit other indie stores when I travel. After fourteen years in the business, I continue to learn from people in those other stores, and they often recommend books I wouldn't have thought of reading or giving as gifts.

The timing on Indies First was also just right. Most of us manage to muddle along finding good things to read for ourselves. But finding good books as gifts can be more challenging. That's where the perspective of the authors helps. They can come up with ideas for gift-giving that the store staff might not have thought of. Right before Christmas, that's invaluable.

I owe a big thank you to Sherman Alexie for coming up with the idea, to the American Booksellers Association for promoting it, and to Craig Lancaster for bringing it to my store. It made a difference to us. You can make a difference at your local store, too.

By joining in at Indies First, you're in a low-pressure environment where nobody expects you to be drawing the crowd. Shopping is heavy that day anyway, and the people visiting the store are book lovers who support independent stores. You'll have a chance to talk with other authors and watch how they handle the event, and perhaps to make contacts for future events.

In my store, Indies First 2015 had overlapping schedules that guaranteed at least three authors in the store at all times (not counting myself). Except for the first and last time slots of the day, each author overlapped with different people at the beginning and end of their time, typically connecting with four other authors. I wanted it to be as much a networking opportunity for them as a marketing opportunity for the store.

Matching up authors

There are two ways to match up authors for a multi-author event: the authors can do it or the venue can do it.

If you have a writer friend that shares a genre, style, or setting with you, consider doing a tour together. It makes for a better deal for the store, as they'll probably draw a bigger crowd and sell more books, and it gives each author a chance to draw from the other's fan base.

Mark Spragg (author of *Where Rivers Change Direction*, *An Unfinished Life*, and other books) is a perennial favorite in my town. When the 2010 release date was announced for his book *Bone Fire*, I called him about setting up a launch event. Mark told me that a friend of his, Laura Bell, had her first novel, *Claiming Ground*, coming out at the same time from the same publisher. He suggested we make it a double appearance.

The response was so strong that we moved the readings across the street to the Elks Club. Both authors came into the store and signed books for an hour, and then we gave them a short break before starting the party at the Elks. The place was packed and festive—we even had cakes made that were decorated to look like the book covers.

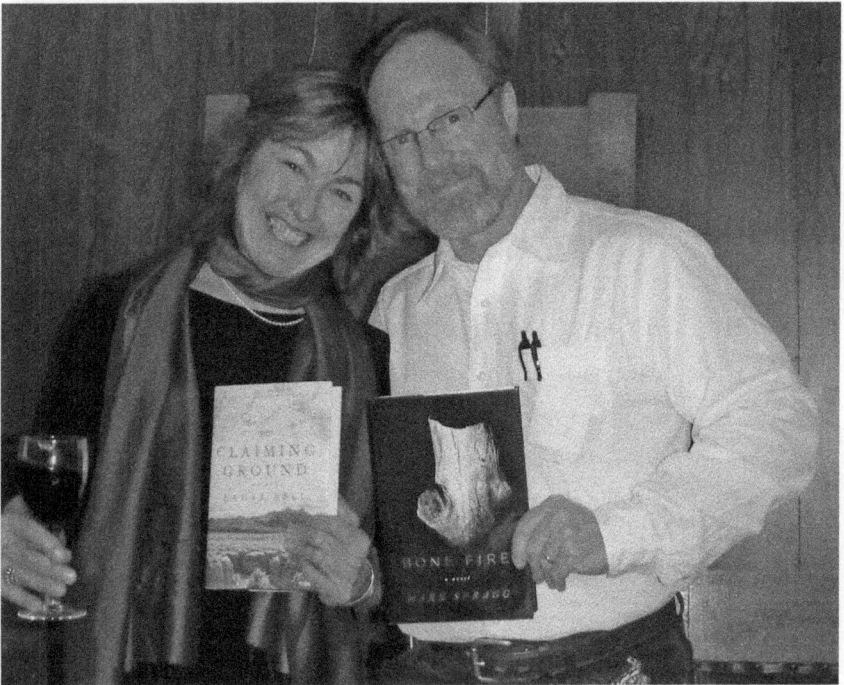

Both Mark and Laura ended up selling more books than either would have by themselves. That kind of symbiosis is invaluable.

Tips & Tricks From the Pros

As often as possible, try to pair an established author with a newer author for the event. That way, the new author doesn't face an empty room and benefits from the status of the more successful author. Two of the most enjoyable events I was part of were at the Poisoned Pen in Scottsdale, AZ, when I was paired with Nevada Barr and later with C.J. Box. Mystery/suspense authors in my experience are very generous with sharing a stage, and they enjoy sharing it in the sense that they are not all alone making the same presentation they've made a hundred times before. Authors can be egotistical as hell, but even the most egotistical can eventually get sick of their own stories. It also helps to have the two authors conduct interviews with each other, asking questions.

Keith McCafferty, award-winning author of *Crazy Mountain Kiss* and the rest of the Sean Stranahan series.

This is also a great way for a well-known author to give a boost to someone lesser known. Craig Johnson (author of the bestselling Walt Longmire series) toured with another mystery writer named C. M. Wendelboe (author of the Manny Tanno mysteries). Craig was a huge phenomenon at the time, with his book series being turned into the top drama on A&E, and he could draw a crowd anywhere. By taking a friend along with him, it gave bookstores and Longmire fans alike a look at a new mystery writer, and did well for everyone. I wasn't familiar with the Manny Tanno books at the time, but they have been selling steadily for us ever since that event.

If the store is arranging the event, a similar strategy applies.

Rule number one for bookstores setting up multi-author events: never schedule two authors at the same time without talking to both of them first. You can't assume that all authors are best buddies. Sometimes writers don't get along with each other, and sometimes there's a long history behind the animosity. The last thing you want is two authors sniping at each other in the store and making the customers feel uncomfortable.

Panel discussions

As authors, we all have those moments when we want the spotlight all to ourselves. We also tend to be generally busy people, especially if we have other jobs along with our writing careers, and this can discourage us from going to panel discussions.

I've been on a variety of panels over the years, both as the moderator and as one of the panelists. Every one of them has given me an opportunity to learn from other authors, and most of them have introduced me to some wonderful people.

Tales from the Front Lines

Perhaps my most memorable reading/signing was when I attended a Duran Duran fan convention in Chicago three years ago. I wrote a memoir (*Friends of Mine: Thirty Years in the Life of a Duran Duran Fan*) about my thirty-year fan experience, and I was on a panel with other authors. We each took a turn reading an excerpt from and discussing our book, followed by a Q&A and signing. I sold out my entire stock and had to take names and addresses for those unfortunate to be at the end of the line when I ran out! But I followed up and sent each person a signed book within the week. It was a lot of fun, and my reading was well-received, especially with a lot of laughs, as was intended. How you read and present your excerpt makes a real difference.

Elisa Lorello, author of *Faking It*, *She Has Your Eyes*, *Ordinary World*, and other works.

Panel discussion are invigorating and sometimes humbling for an author. Years ago, I was invited to participate on a panel about writing science and nature themes for children. I was seated next to Sneed B. Collard. He probably had three times as many children's books out as I did, covering a wider range of topics and published by some very big publishing companies. I was intimidated, but he and the other panelists were welcoming and encouraging and it became a great learning experience for me.

It doesn't matter whether you're a participant or a moderator; panels are one of the few places that you can learn, teach, and network all at the same time — and get exposure while you're doing it. Any time you are asked to be on a panel, go for it!

When you show up for the panel discussion, you can't count on having anything on the table in front of you aside from a microphone, which you might have to share. I recommend bringing along many of the same things you'd bring to a book signing:

- A bottle of water, because talking a lot can make you thirsty.
- A copy of your book — and copies of older books if you've published more than one. Don't bring stacks of books; you aren't there to sell. Just bring one to put on the table in front of you. If it's not a book that stands up well by itself, bring a stand. People may have trouble keeping track of which author on the panel wrote which book, and a copy of the book will help them keep it straight.
- A stack of business cards or bookmarks to hand out to anyone who comes up after the discussion to chat with you.
- A prop. It doesn't matter what it is, as long as it relates to your book or your look (persona). Like the copy of your book, its purpose is to sit on the table in front of you and reinforce in people's heads which author you are.

Sometimes the props can lead to entertaining photos, which spread farther and faster on social media than the usual boring photograph of a smiling author holding up a book. I was on a children's book panel at the High Plains Book Festival a couple of years ago, and the author next to me was Marion Mutala, with a book called *Baba's Babushka, A Magical Ukrainian Wedding*.

As her prop, Marion had a babushka (head scarf) like the one in her book. I didn't have a book prop, but I did have my trademark cowboy hat, which is part of my look at book events. She and I swapped headgear for a photo, and it ended up being one of the most popular pictures either of us posted from the event.

The only existing photograph of me wearing a babushka,
and probably the only one of Marion Mutala in a cowboy hat.

Since my cowboy hats are part of my trademark "look" (see "Develop a look" on page 6) I've had a bunch of authors borrow it or swap hats with me when we got our pictures together. If your fans want a picture with you, make it a fun picture!

If you are a panelist, ask in advance if they can tell you what the discussion topics will be. Sometimes they'll even give you a prepared list of questions so you can have an answer ready at hand.

If you are a moderator, make sure you put together a list of questions and topics that suits the panelists and the event. You never know whether you'll have panelists that give short, sweet answers one sentence long; or whether the panelists will go on at great detail, taking five minutes to answer a simple question.

Part of your job as the moderator is to keep things moving, but you don't want to cut off the panelists every time they answer a question, so write more questions than you'll have a chance to use and prioritize them. If things are going quickly, use them all. If things are moving slowly, skip the lower-priority questions.

Book Conferences and Festivals

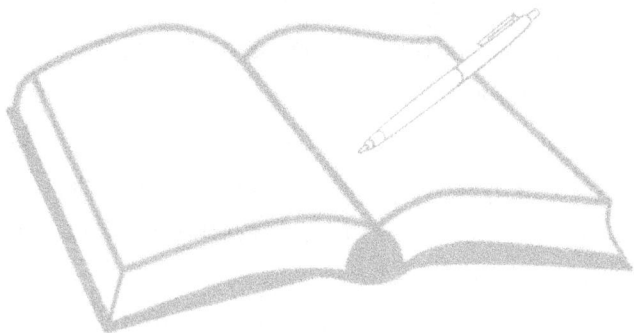

CHAPTER 12

The most amazing signing I ever had was in Portland, Oregon in 2013. I had a huge line, and was moving people through at a rate of one every 40 seconds until we ran out of books. It was exhilarating! It made me feel like a rock star! It also didn't make me a dime in royalties.

The signing was at a Pacific Northwest Booksellers Association conference, and all of the books were donated by my publisher. Like every other publisher on the planet, they don't pay authors a royalty on promotional copies that they give away for free.

Luckily, I wasn't there to earn royalties on those books. I was there to put copies of my book in the hands of bookstore owners and employees. I shook their hands, I handed out business cards, I gave them free books, and I offered to come to their stores. The process is called networking, and it's extraordinarily effective. In fact, shows like that are where I've met many of the authors who later signed books in my store, and many of the people who provided tips and anecdotes for this book.

Every book show is different. Some are easy to get into and some are invitation only. Some have huge trade show floors and some are purely educational conferences with networking events. There are a few things they have in common, though:

Publishers are usually expected to pay to get their authors in the door. If you're a self-published author, that expense is all yours.

Similarly, conferences rarely pay for travel or lodging for the authors, unless your name happens to be J. K. Rowling or Stephen King, in which case you probably aren't reading this book. It's between you and your publisher to get you there. That's one of the reasons it makes sense to look for shows near you.

Most associations reward persistence. The first time you show up, you might be an unknown author, and they'll put you in the back of a cocktail party with 40 other authors. The next time, you may graduate to a scheduled appearance or a "meet the author" breakfast. Keep showing up (and keep writing books), and you may be one of the meal speakers or give a keynote address.

At bookseller conferences, publishers are expected to donate books. At literary conferences or book festivals, attendees usually pay for their books, which makes it more like an appearance at a store.

Until you're well established and have a hot book on the market, you'll be sharing the spotlight with other authors. Lots of other authors. Don't compete with them for attention. Be the one that gets along with everybody and helps out anywhere you can. That gets you invited back, and it also gives you a good reputation with your fellow authors.

Exhibit tables and booths

One of the big draws of a convention is the exhibit floor. Book buyers can go from booth to booth discovering new books, new authors, new publishers, new sidelines, and new distributors.

Being visible on the exhibit floor is a good way to get yourself out in front of people who are at the show to spend money. Some will place orders on the spot, and others may take a brochure and talk to you later. If your book is available through the big distributors (Ingram, Baker & Taylor, Partners…), book buyers may just add your books to their next distribution order.

This makes it a bit difficult to judge the cost effectiveness of the show. You can't just add up the costs of attending — travel, hotel, booth space, free giveaways — and subtract from the orders received at the show. If you're doing it right, orders will be coming in weeks and months after the show is over, and orders from distributors will increase as well.

Signage

No matter what approach you take, you'll need some kind of signage. If you've been doing book signings, you can start with whatever you already have (see "Posters & signs" on page 19), but remember this isn't a bookstore that's focused on you for the day. You are one of many exhibitors, and you are on your own for equipment. If you have a poster, take an easel. If you have a tabletop sign, make sure it has a stand. If you bring a banner, bring a way to hang it! Also, when you have your banner made, make sure it has grommets on the corners and top-center to hang it from.

Table drapes are inexpensive and look nice. They're basically tablecloths designed to hang over the front of the table. The front part that hangs over the front can have your name and book info screen-printed on it, or you can clip a banner to it. At a crowded show, you don't want this to be your only signage, because nobody can read it when there's a group of people in front of your table — and hopefully there will *always* be a group of people in front of your table!

Setting up your own table or booth

If you are setting up your own table, you need to be prepared. Get all of the details in advance about what the conference provides and what you need to provide.

A typical single-table exhibit space will include the table (covered & draped) and one or two chairs. You may or may not have a backdrop.

A typical booth will have an eight-foot pipe-and-drape backdrop behind you and possibly short pipe-and-drape dividers between your booth and the ones to either side. It may or may not include tables and chairs, although one table and two chairs is common. In smaller venues like a hotel ballroom, you'll have a nice carpeted floor. In larger venues like a convention center, you may have to bring your own carpet or rent one if you don't want to be on a concrete floor.

Finding out what's included in advance is critical. Make sure you have all of your supplies (see "Your Exhibitor Kit" on page 137). You don't want to be scrambling around trying to find a pen or a safety pin when everybody else is already set up and selling.

Make sure you know how much space you have to work with. Booth spaces might be ten feet wide or eight feet wide. Your table may be eight foot or six foot — or you may be getting half of an eight foot table, with another author next to you.

Sharing a table

In the book *How to Make Webcomics*, Brad Guigar recommends that on the first day you should "bring a box of a dozen donuts to share with your neighbors. It's a great way to get off on the right foot with your fellow exhibitors. Once you've plied them with a

Your Exhibitor Kit

I usually use a toolbox or tackle box for my show kit, but I've seen others use a briefcase, tote bag, or cardboard box. Be sure to have a list of what's supposed to be in the kit so that you can replenish it each time you set up for a show.

- S-hook fasteners for hanging banners on backdrops

- Miscellaneous fasteners (paper clips, safety pins, zip ties, string, fishing line, rubber bands, push pins...)

- Duct tape. Don't go anywhere without duct tape!

- Transparent tape (both a small roll for fixing or attaching signs and a big roll in case you have to seal a box)

- Pens. Lots of pens. Whatever you sign with and a big Sharpie

- Book stands

- A notepad and a pad or two of Post-Its

- Scissors and a knife

- A pair of pliers, small hammer, and a couple of screwdrivers

- Extra business cards

- Quick & dirty first-aid kit (band-aids, aspirin, lip balm, tweezers...)

- A flash drive containing artwork for anything you're handing out, so you can print more at the nearest copy shop

- Some emergency drinks & snacks, because sometimes you can't get away from the table long enough to get lunch

- If you have any electronics, take at least one extension cord and/or power strip—and an extra phone charger can't hurt

- A pack or small box of tissues

little sugar, you'll be able to count on them for anything as the convention wears on."

It sounds a bit mercenary, but Brad is absolutely right. Be the one that brings donuts, that has a push pin when someone else needs one, that's willing to help lift a heavy box. If you're the nice guy, then your fellow exhibitors will be there for you when you need them.

If you are sharing a table, make sure to get there early to set up your space, keeping it all in your allotted area. That way if there's a problem of any kind, you'll have time to fix it. Also, once you're set up, it's harder for your table-mate to sprawl into your area.

Appearing at your publisher's table

When your publisher offers you a spot in their booth, it is typically for a specific time slot. They may set aside a three or four-foot area and rotate several authors through it.

Be there early for your time slot, but don't pressure the previous author. Keep to your allotted space, and remember you are appearing at the pleasure of your publisher: be helpful and cooperative, pull people to their table, and you'll be invited back.

Selling books

At some shows, you're there to show off your book, talk about it, and possibly give away free samples. At other shows, you are there to sell books. In the latter situation, take along plenty of books. It's far better to have to lug back some boxes at the end of the conference than to run out and lose sales.

Displaying the books

Even though it's a pain in the neck to unpack and repack boxes, do it! Pull those books out and stack 'em up on the table. Have at least one on a book stand so that people walking on the other side of the aisle can see it, but pile the rest up.

People are much more likely to buy from a huge stack of books than pick up one of two copies. Whether they're subconsciously thinking, *look at all those books! This must be really popular!* or whether they just don't like taking one of the last copies, this approach works. As booksellers say, "stack 'em high and watch 'em fly."

Taking money

You see plenty of booths that take cash only or credit cards only. My philosophy is that I want to make it as easy as possible for potential customers to give me money.

For cash sales, round off the price of the book and back out taxes. You don't want to deal with change. If you have a $19.99 book, round the price off to $20 for the show (but carry a penny or two just for the smart-alec who wants his change).

If you have a $24.95 book at a trade conference where you'd normally offer a 40% discount, which would be $14.97, just tell people it's a flat $15 at the show.

If you have to collect 8% tax on a $12.50 book, just round it off to $13, include the tax, and eat the extra 50¢.

For checks, figure out your policy in advance. Will you accept only business checks, only checks below a certain dollar value, only local checks, or no checks at all? As time goes on, this becomes less and less of an issue; almost everyone carries a credit card or debit card these days.

For cards, sign up with one of the merchant card systems that runs on your phone or tablet. I picked Square because they have no monthly fees and the magnetic stripe reader is free. There are plenty of other options, though, so do some homework and see what works best for you.

Pick a company that supports contactless (also called NFC or near-field communication) payment systems like Apple Pay and Android Pay as well. With those systems, all the customer has to do is place their phone within a few inches of your reader and confirm the payment.

Selling books on credit

At the professional shows, you will probably be approached by someone who says, "This looks great. I'll take five. Ship them to my store and bill me."

Be prepared with a policy and an invoice form.

If you're going to accept orders on credit, decide what the terms will be in advance. Most publishers offer net 30, which means the store has 30 days to pay after they receive the invoice. Others may shorten it to net 10. You can offer an incentive for paying early; net 30 terms with 2% net 10 added on mean that the store can pay you the full amount in 30 days, or pay in 10 days or less and take a 2% discount.

Decide also what the shipping terms are. You don't want to be scrambling around trying to figure out what shipping costs while there's someone standing in front of you with a Visa card trying to buy 50 books from you. Weigh out some of your books in advance and check with UPS or the Post Office to see what shipping costs for one, three, five, or ten books, and make a wholesale shipping and discount chart. It might look like this:

1–4 books: 20% discount, $5 freight

5–9 books: 40% discount, $10 freight

10+ books: 40% discount, free freight

There's nothing wrong with requiring that show orders be paid up front. Conference attendees carry credit cards for just that reason!

Non-Book Trade Shows

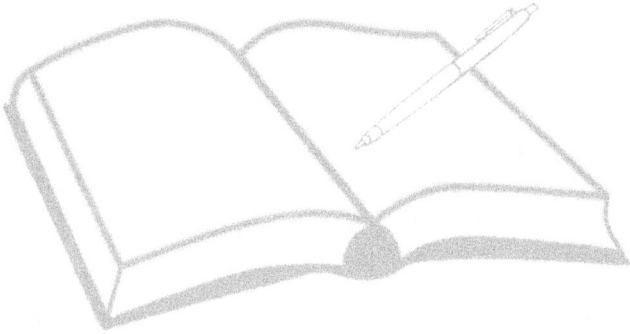

CHAPTER 13

The very first book signing I ever did was at a technical conference for court reporters in 1996. My co-author, Richard Sherman, and I were taking turns manning a table near the conference registration area by the main hallway. There was another table next to ours where a fellow named Richard Lederer was peddling his books, including *Anguished English*, *Get Thee to a Punnery*, and *Crazy English*.

I sat down behind my table with a stack of books in front of me and watched the crowds of people streaming by. A few stopped to see what I was up to and take a peek at my book, *The Court Reporter's Guide to Cyberspace*. As I sat there meekly waiting for the world to cut a path to my door, Richard Lederer was putting the "crazy" in *Crazy English*.

The man never stopped moving, never sat down. He was on his feet, greeting people, telling them jokes, asking them questions, and putting copies of his book in their hands.

He worked the crowd like a busker in Times Square, and he sold a lot of books.

As soon as things quieted down—I think a seminar had started—Richard came over to my table and introduced himself. He handed me a copy of one of his books, and absentmindedly flipped through mine.

He told me that if I ever expected to sell books at a conference, I'd better get up off my butt and talk to people. "Look at their badges," he said, "and make a comment about the town they live in or the business they work for."

As an aside, when you attend a conference, please don't wear your badge on your hip or a very long lanyard. It makes it very awkward for a tall guy like me to read the badge!

During the next few hours, whenever there weren't potential customers in the halls, he coached me on selling books at trade shows. Time that he could have spent relaxing, he spent with me instead.

His advice stuck with me. I didn't rise to his level of flamboyancy at that show, but I have gone to many more shows over the years and I've learned from his lessons. The most important of those is to be visible. I have a bit of an advantage there, being 6'5" tall, but I lose that advantage sitting down. Now I stand up and move around, and if there's nobody at my table, I'll wander off and start up conversations with people (watching my table out of the corner of my eye, of course).

Giving a talk at a trade show

If you've been invited to talk at a trade show, it's because you have something interesting to say or to teach. Your book gives you credibility, but it's not the main thing bringing people in the door.

Draw content from the book. Mention the book. But don't make your talk all about the book, and don't turn your talk into a sales pitch for the book. If you give a compelling speech, your book will only need to be mentioned twice: once by the person who introduces you, and once at the end of your presentation when you bring up a slide with a picture of your book cover on it and mention you'll be signing books in the lobby in five minutes.

Speaking of which, where should you have your book signing table? When there's a small crowd (50 or fewer people), I typically have a table in the back of the room where somebody can sell books. I move to that table immediately following my talk and sign books until we run out of people, run out of books, or get chased out of the room so they can set up for the next session.

When there's a larger audience, this can get awkward. Crowds can block the door, and the conference organizers want to get in and clean up the room. In those cases, it's better to have a spot outside the room designated for the signing. Make sure it's easy to find, and that someone is there ahead of you setting everything up.

My largest conference audience was about 630 people. The trade association set up my signing table across the lobby from the table where they were selling copies of my *Closed Captioning Handbook*. This allowed people who already had a copy to bypass the sales line, and provided plenty of room for a signing line that was out of the way of the book sales table.

Other speakers, typically the more well-known ones, may take a different approach, eliminating the signing table entirely. In 1992, I attended a seminar by William Gallagher, co-author of *Guerrilla Selling: Unconventional Weapons and Tactics for Increasing Your Sales*. They didn't need a book sales table, as they had built the cost of his book into the fee for the event.

When we walked into the room, each chair had a copy of the book and some other promotional materials sitting on it. We had an opportunity to go up after the event to meet Bill and have him sign books.

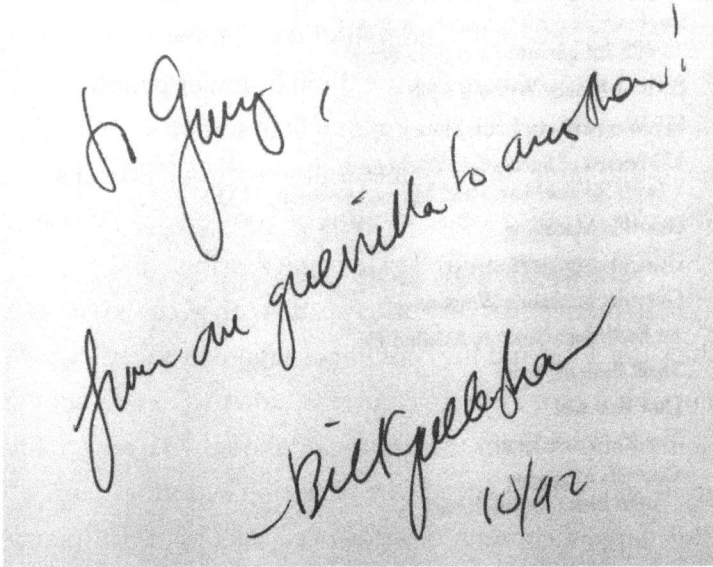

*Gallagher showed good form here, dating his signature
and adding a clever tag line that ties into the book title.*

Speakers disagree about the wisdom of distributing books before the event. Some feel that it removes the bottleneck after the talk and allows people to follow along in the book where appropriate. Others, myself included, feel that the audience will be distracted looking through the book rather than paying attention to the speech.

If your appearance is sponsored by a bookstore that's handling your book sales, don't forget to thank them. Yes, they are making money from the books, but putting a thank-you slide in your presentation and mentioning them by name during the talk is a classy move that doesn't cost you a thing.

It also generates good PR with the store, which they just may remember next time it comes to sponsoring an event for you. Here's the closing slide from a presentation I did at the National Bighorn Sheep Center in Dubois, Wyoming in 2012:

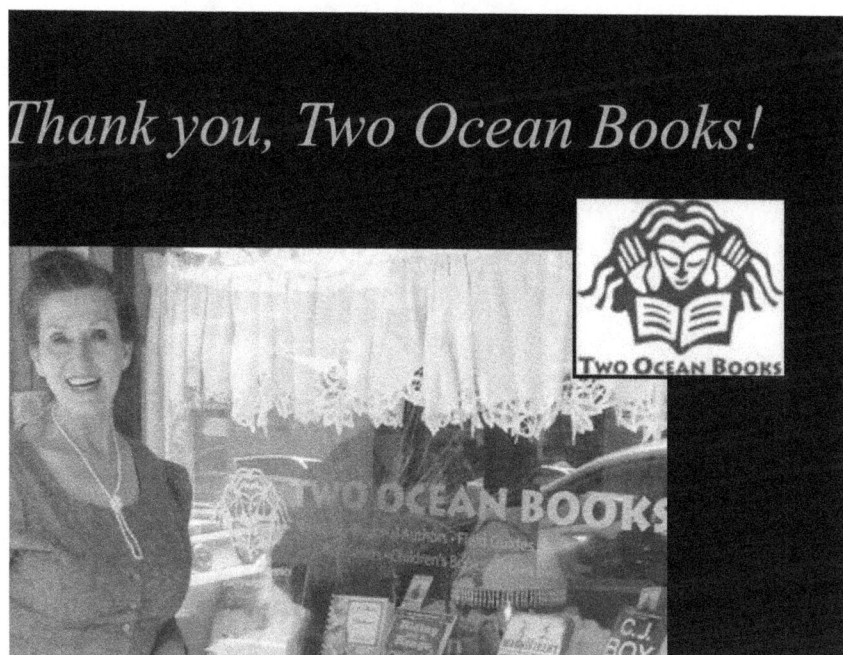

This slide pictures Julie Kosmata Elliott in front of her store, Two Ocean Books, which tragically burned to the ground in December of 2014.

It's usually easy to grab the bookstore's logo from their website. If you can grab a picture like this of the owner of the store, it makes the "thank you" even more personal and memorable.

Working social media at a live event

In 2011, I was doing a book signing event at the National Court Reporters Association (NCRA) annual conference. At their booth, directly across from my book signing table, they had a big projection screen showing three Twitter feeds.

As I dealt with customers, the tweets scrolled by in my peripheral vision. I didn't look closely until the next conference sessions began and all of the attendees filed off into seminar rooms. At that point, I realized that the screen was showing tweets from the association's official Twitter feed: both tweets directed to the association, and tweets containing the official hashtag for the conference (#NCRA11).

After watching the feed scroll by for a while, I got curious. I asked the association if they'd announce a free book for the first person who mentioned the tweet. I figured I might get someone as soon as the current sessions were over. They sent out the tweet, and I immediately retweeted it.

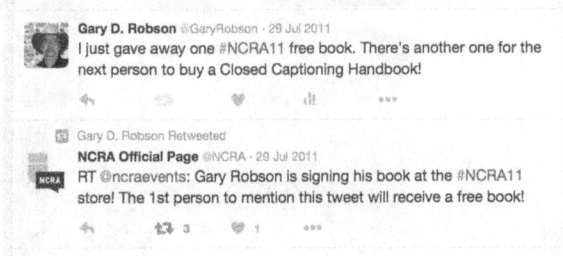

Gary D. Robson @GaryRobson · 29 Jul 2011
I just gave away one #NCRA11 free book. There's another one for the next person to buy a Closed Captioning Handbook!

Gary D. Robson Retweeted
NCRA Official Page @NCRA · 29 Jul 2011
RT @ncraevents: Gary Robson is signing his book at the #NCRA11 store! The 1st person to mention this tweet will receive a free book!

In less than a minute, the door of one of the seminar rooms quietly opened and someone slipped out. I assumed she was on her way to the restroom, but she was heading straight for my table, cell phone in hand.

After she showed me the tweet on her phone and collected her book, I felt a bit guilty for pulling her out of the session. But hey, she's the one that was checking Twitter while the presentation was going on. So I did it again. This time offering a free copy of one of my older books to the next person who bought my newer one.

Another door opened. Then another. Five people got up in the middle of a seminar and walked out to buy a book. I feel guilty for that little experiment now, as I was dragging people out of other people's presentations, but I learned something that day about the power of real-time social media.

When you're sitting at your book signing table and don't have a customer to engage, go ahead and pull that phone out and hit Facebook, Twitter, or Instagram. It just might sell you some books.

Creative marketing opportunities

Sometimes you have to be opportunistic. See a possibility and grab it.

One example is an opportunity that isn't going to come up very often for most authors. I was checking in to the Old Faithful Inn in Yellowstone National Park, where I'd be signing my *Who Pooped in the Park?* books in the lobby the next morning. There is no Wi-Fi available there — even cell service is sketchy at best. I noticed people checking their phones for Wi-Fi and asking at the registration desk where they could get Internet access.

When we checked in and went to our room, we found that there was no Wi-Fi available in the hotel except for "Dave's iPhone." I don't know who Dave is, but he had a password on his Wi-Fi, so it didn't do us any good.

Luckily, however, I have my iPhone set up to become a mobile Wi-Fi hot spot, too. Using it for that does suck the juice out of the battery, so I don't use it that often, but this situation gave me an idea . There was only one visible Wi-Fi network in the hotel, and it would probably be going away soon. So I changed the name of my iPhone and activated the mobile hot-spot app (with a good secure password) when my signing began the next morning. What did people see when they searched for a Wi-Fi hot spot that day?

Wi-Fi

Wi-Fi   ON

Choose a Network...

✓ Who Pooped? In the lobby!

Other...   >

Ask to Join Networks   ON

Known networks will be joined automatically. If no known networks are available, you will be asked before joining a new network.

I really have no idea whether it sold any books that day, but it definitely got some chuckles, and I'm hoping everyone that saw it will remember it.

Gary D. Robson

Where Are We Going In This Handbasket?

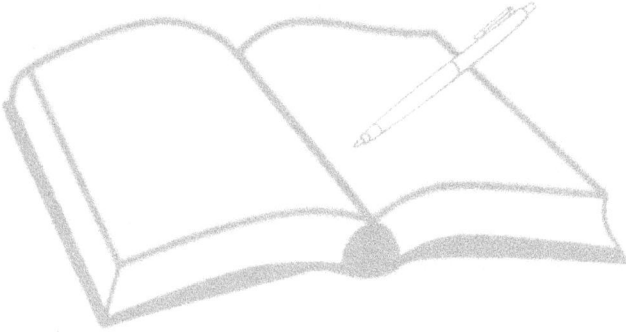

CHAPTER 14

If you get out there and do book signings, the law of averages says that some of them will be good and some will be the event from Hell (handbasket optional). All kinds of things can go wrong, whether you're Stephen King or an unknown writer doing your first event.

I don't have nearly enough hubris to say that I've seen it all, or had it all happen to me, but I've seen quite a few situations go south. The wrong cable to connect my computer to their projector, so I couldn't use my PowerPoint presentation. Showing up when I thought I was just doing a book signing but they thought I was giving a half-hour talk (it's improv time!). Having no books.

I was scheduled to give a talk in Yellowstone National Park, and I had planned to arrive an hour in advance. Then traffic stopped. It didn't slow down, it stopped entirely. We sat for over 15 minutes without moving, during which time

I realized that (a) I was probably going to be late, (b) there was no cell service, so I couldn't call and tell them, and (c) I really shouldn't have had that great big huge iced tea.

People were getting out of their cars and wandering about, so I did the same. When a car finally came by going the other direction, I hollered "how far does this mess go?" The driver said "ten miles."

At that point, I hustled off into the trees to deal with the iced tea situation, hoping that I'd make it back to the car before things started moving. I needn't have worried.

As it turned out, a small herd of bison had wandered onto the road at the mouth of a canyon. There was a cliff on one side of the road and a river on the other, so there was no way for the bison to get off the road or for drivers to go around them. It took the rangers over an hour to convince the bison to leave the canyon and get off the road.

I was late, but they understood. These things happen in the wilderness. Anywhere else, it could have been a flat tire, an accident on the road, or a late plane.

The best thing to do in situations like this is to have a backup plan and keep a positive attitude. Stress is contagious. If the bookstore staff and the author can appear relaxed, it can help keep the crowd calm and the situation under control.

Tales from the Front Lines

Worst experience I ever had was at a Wal-Mart in Polson. They shoved aside a couple racks of pastels in the ladies plus-size section and parked me behind a card table across from the McDonald's. There was a plastic Ronald McDonald sitting on a bench, mimicking my posture, and doing a lot more business than I was.

Scott McMillion, author of *Mark of the Grizzly*.

Tales from the Front Lines

In a town in Washington that shall remain unnamed, I had three people show up; one of them turned out to be a heckler, who'd come to harass one of the other two people, a judge, for a divorce ruling the judge had made. I actually had to tell the fellow that we'd come together to have a conversation about wilderness and grief, and that I'd appreciate it if he could wait until we were through to bring up his stuff with the judge. This was echoed by a staff member, at which point the guy left (leaving me with two people!)

Gary Ferguson, author of over a dozen books, including *The Carry Home*, *Through the Woods*, and *Hawks Rest*.

I have been on the opposite side of the "late author" situation, too. Greg Mortenson was scheduled for an event in my store in 2007 right after the release of the paperback edition of *Three Cups of Tea*. It was at the height of his popularity, and we had publicized the bejeebers out of the event. He was late.

It's hard to keep an upbeat attitude in a packed store when the guest of honor is an hour late. The line of impatient fans went all the way out the door and halfway down the block. Luckily, we had scheduled an informal book signing before his talk, so that people who just wanted to grab a book didn't have to attend the talk if they didn't want to. This gave us a little bit more flexibility on time.

We did our best to entertain the crowd, gave out some free stuff, and pushed the talk back half an hour so he'd have time to sign books for everyone in line.

When Greg arrived, he was tired and stressed, but he took a deep breath, put on a smile, and dealt with everybody graciously and pleasantly. He also gave us a stack of hardcover copies of his book to give away.

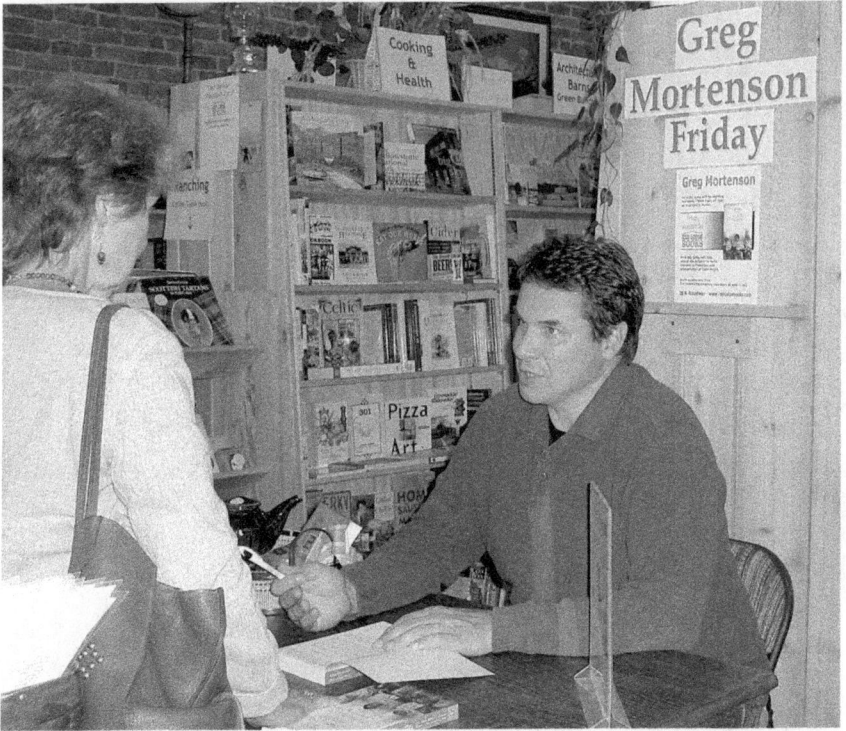

Even if you're hurrying to get through a long line, it's important not to make the customers feel rushed. Here, Greg Mortenson is talking with each person and making eye contact, so that everyone in line feels like they made a personal connection.

There are any number of things that authors and booksellers can do wrong, but even more that are completely out of everyone's control. At times like that, you just need to look at it as a great story to tell and move on.

Guilt? At a book event?

Guilt can also be a side effect of a bad situation. *New York Times* bestselling author James W. Hall is best known for his Thorn series, but he also put out a book called *Hot Damn!*, which is filled with humorous essays. Among those are a few tales from book tours, and he graciously allowed me to reprint one of them here.

Tales from the Front Lines

I was in Saint Paul, Minnesota, a couple of winters ago. January, noon, downtown at a Barnes & Noble. It was a dreary twenty-four degrees, and there were some drizzles of snow mingled with the exhaust fumes and the razory wind. Another cheery moment on the glamorous book tour.

After wandering around for half an hour in the numbing cold searching for the bookstore, I finally found it and went inside. As soon as I defrosted, I located the special-events coordinator and introduced myself as the speaker for the day. She was a cordial young lady, and after a little chitchat about the weather (she thought it was a pretty nice day), she led me over to their reading corner, where there were twenty or so comfortable chairs spread around the small podium where I would make my edifying remarks, hoping to stimulate a frenzy of impulse buying of my latest novel.

Lo and behold, the chairs were filled. A noontime crowd of twenty or so people, a little scruffy-looking, perhaps, but fans nonetheless. My heart leaped up to think that somehow enthusiasm for my south Florida thrillers had penetrated to these icy climes. All these people had decided to take an hour out of their lives so that I could entertain them.

The special-events lady went back to her main desk and made an announcement over the store's PA system that the author James W. Hall had arrived and would shortly give a reading of his work in the west alcove.

Even as the echo of her voice was dying out, each and every person occupying the comfy chairs of the reading area stood up, pulled on his or her heavy coat, and filed toward the exit.

I was speechless. And audienceless.

When the special-events lady came back to join me, I asked what in the world had happened to my audience.

"Oh, they're street people," she said. "We let them come in out of the cold, but they know the drill. When an author shows up, they have to give up their seats."

Not only had I lost my crowd, but I had exiled a host of desperate souls back out to the frigid streets. Was anything I had to say worth that?

For the next hour I hung around and talked to my two legitimate Saint Paul fans and tried to keep from looking out the large windows, where the street people were milling around, slapping their arms, casting frequent looks into the store to see if the visiting writer had left yet.

Ah, yes. Just one more stop on the great ego-adjustment tour.

James W. Hall, author of *Hot Damn!*.

It is easy to forget sometimes what draws people to your event. Each year, I sign books in the lobby of the Old Faithful Inn in Yellowstone National Park. For those unfamiliar with the inn, it gets its name from Yellowstone's biggest attraction, the Old Faithful Geyser, which is right outside. It is an amazingly predictable geyser, going off about once every hour and a half.

The Old Faithful Inn itself is quite a wonder. It is the largest log cabin ever built, with an awe-inspiring six-story high lobby made entirely from local trees a hundred years ago. And that lobby is where they place my table.

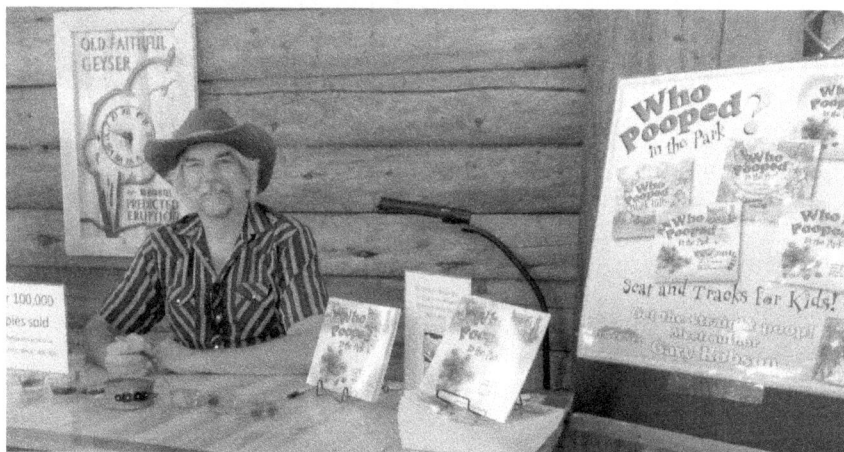

Here I sit, ready to become the center of attention!

On my first visit, I settled in at my seat, arranged the table to my liking, and waited to be mobbed by adoring fans. I didn't have long to wait before the lobby was filled with throngs of people, and all of them were looking my way!

Each time someone came over to the table, I greeted them politely, but most of them avoided eye contact, glanced at their watch, and wandered off. It didn't dawn on me at first that they weren't actively avoiding eye contact; they were looking just over my right shoulder at the clock that shows the next eruption time.

It wasn't long before someone engaged with me. She walked directly up to the table, glanced at the sign next to the table, looked me in the eye, and said, "Where's the bathroom?"

Ego-adjustment tour, indeed.

Tales from the Front Lines

Folks such as Duane Wilkins at University Book Store in Seattle are wonderful, but others don't always communicate so well. There was the other bookstore where I turned up for the signing and not only had the signing been cancelled, but the manager hadn't ordered any stock (to sign for later) and wouldn't come out of her office to talk to me. The clerk didn't actually say "The store is closing forever," but I wasn't surprised when I read a short time later that it had closed.

Vonda McIntyre, Hugo and Nebula award-winning science fiction author.

My Yellowstone signings are some of my favorites. I look forward to visiting the Park every year. But it does take some getting used to.

Several years later, I was back in the Old Faithful Inn and had an entirely different kind of disaster.

It was about 6:15 p.m., and I had been sitting at that table since 11:00 (minus a few bathroom breaks). I was chatting with a family when an alarm sounded. I made some quip about someone opening a door they shouldn't have opened, and then a recorded voice came on asking everyone to evacuate the hotel. The restaurant was full, with a line halfway through the lobby. The bar was full. The gift shop was packed. There were lines at registration. People were unpacking their bags in their rooms. Everyone began streaming out.

I had my handy-dandy leather satchel with me, so I swiftly stuffed my important possessions in it (signing pen, props, phone) and headed outside. The books and the sign were left to fend for themselves.

Cell service at the Old Faithful Inn is spotty. Did I say "spotty"? I really meant "lousy." In the interests of keeping Yellowstone as pristine as possible, there is one cell tower in the area, and it is utterly incapable of handling the data traffic that people attempt to use it for. When I went outside, I found myself surrounded by hundreds of people all trying — with varying degrees of success — to tweet about the experience. I managed to get a tweet to go through myself, shot a text message to my wife so she could find me, and then settled in to chat with people.

"We had just gotten our dinner," one woman lamented. "I had only had one bite of my steak!"

"There's the difference between men and women," I told her. "I would have brought the steak with me."

In general, people handled the situation with grace and humor. Someone commented that a vendor with a beer cart would be making a mint. Someone else said if there was a fire in the kitchen, at least the food wouldn't get cold.

The signing was scheduled to end at 7:00, and that's about what time we were allowed back in. It wasn't until the next morning that I found out what had actually happened: low water pressure in the fire sprinkler system had triggered the alarm.

I probably lost some sales because of the evacuation, but it's been a fun story to tell.

Tales from the Front Lines

One of the most interesting events I was invited to was Malmstrom Air Force Base in Great Falls, Montana. I was fingerprinted and photographed before being led in a convoy to the store, where I was met by the three organizers of the event and confronted with posters of me that were five feet tall, like I was a visiting royal. The only problem was that there was almost no one in the store, for which the organizers profusely apologized. They couldn't understand it, for the event had been deliberately scheduled to coincide with the busiest time of the week. This mystery was solved when we learned that a mountain lion had been spotted on the base and a Remain In Place order instituted, so that anyone who was planning to come see me was not permitted to leave the building they were in. Eventually, some people did come into the store and I sold more than 50 books, but it could have been many more. When the event was over, I was told to walk directly to my car (there were at least three official vehicles with sirens blaring near the parking lot), after which I was escorted out the back entrance, the front gate having been shut down because of the lion. I thought, this base is in charge of nuclear missile silos. They have sufficient artillery to bring down half of western Europe, and the whole place is brought to a standstill by a cat!

Keith McCafferty, award-winning author of *Crazy Mountain Kiss* and the rest of the Sean Stranahan series.

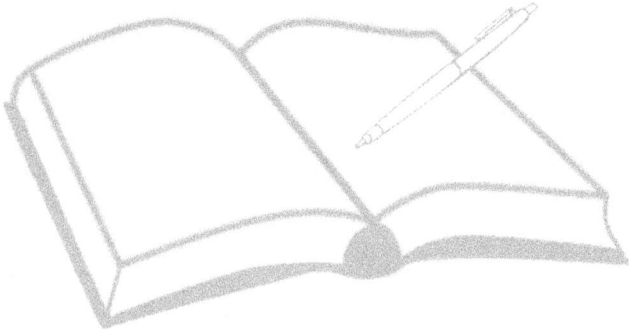

INDEX

A

B

About the Author

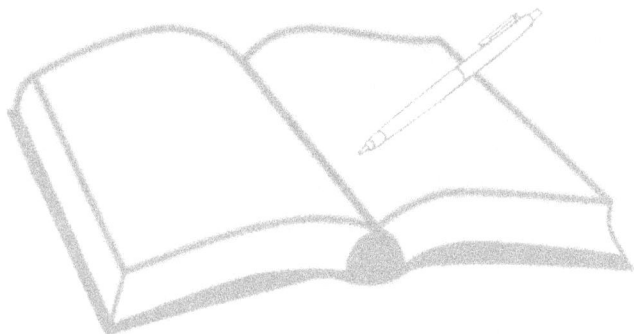

Gary Robson is an author and owner of a bookstore in the booming metropolis of Red Lodge, Montana, population 2,300. He has written over two dozen books, entries for two dictionaries, stories for anthologies, and hundreds of magazine, newspaper, and web articles (and that's not counting blog posts!).

He started out in the technology world and became a vocal advocate of closed captioning on television for deaf and hard-of-hearing people. In his endless quest to figure out what he's going to be when he grows up, he has been granted a couple of patents, teamed up with family members to start an electronics business and a software business, run a small newspaper and a bookstore, taught computer science, written 20 books about poop, raised some cattle, done a little stand-up comedy, put on seminars all over the country, given a TEDx talk, and competed in rodeos.

Luckily for him, Gary's wife and kids are good at smiling tolerantly and putting up with him.

Find out more at Gary's website: GaryDRobson.com.

Other books by Gary D. Robson

Children's Picture Books

Who Pooped in the Black Hills?

Who Pooped in the Cascades?

Who Pooped in Central Park? (New York City)

Who Pooped in the North Woods?

Who Pooped in the Park? (Acadia National Park)

Who Pooped in the Park? (Big Bend National Park)

Who Pooped in the Park? (Death Valley National Park)

Who Pooped in the Park? (Glacier National Park)

Who Pooped in the Park? (Grand Canyon National Park)

Who Pooped in the Park? (Grand Teton National Park)

Who Pooped in the Park? (Olympic National Park)

Who Pooped in the Park? (Red Rock Canyon)

Who Pooped in the Park? (Rocky Mountain National Park)

Who Pooped in the Park? (Sequoia/Kings Canyon National Parks)

Who Pooped in the Park? (Shenandoah National Park)

Who Pooped in the Park? (Yellowstone National Park)

Who Pooped in the Park? (Yosemite National Park)

Who Pooped in the Redwoods?

Who Pooped in the Sonoran Desert?

Who Pooped on the Colorado Plateau?

Technology

The Closed Captioning Handbook

Alternative Realtime Careers

Inside Captioning

The Court Reporter's Guide to Cyberspace, with Richard A. Sherman

Tea

Myths & Legends of Tea

A Tea Journey: Your personal tea cupping journal

History

The Very Best of the Red Lodge Local Rag

The Darkest Hour, with Fay Kuhlman